World Food C

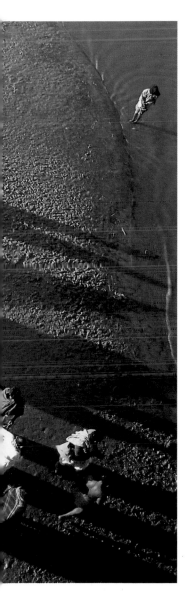

World Food Café

Chris & Carolyn Caldicott

Recipe photography by James Merrell

FRANCES LINCOLN

For Nicholas

Frances Lincoln Limited
4 Torriano Mews
Torriano Avenue
London NW5 2RZ

British Library Cataloguing in Publication Data
A catalogue record for this book is available
from the British Library

ISBN 0 7112 1751 3

Printed in China
First Frances Lincoln Edition 1999
First paperback edition 2002

9 8 7

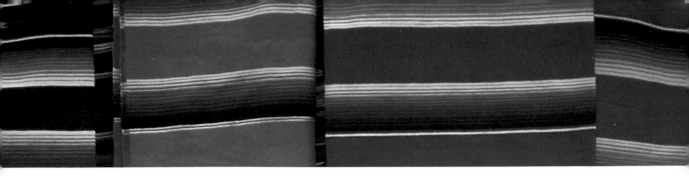

Contents

INTRODUCTION 6

THE MIDDLE EAST & AFRICA	INDIA, NEPAL & SRI LANKA	SOUTHEAST ASIA & CHINA	THE AMERICAS
10	58	112	146

THE MIDDLE EAST & AFRICA
10

Morocco
14

Egypt, Jordan & The Levant
26

Turkey
36

Oman
40

Mali
42

East Africa
46

The Seychelles:
La Digue Island
54

INDIA, NEPAL & SRI LANKA
58

Northern India
62

Eastern India
70

Southern India
76

Western India
86

Nepal
100

Sri Lanka
102

SOUTHEAST ASIA & CHINA
112

Burma
116

China
120

Laos
124

Thailand
128

Malaysia & Indonesia
134

THE AMERICAS
146

Brazil
150

Bolivia
154

Peru
156

Ecuador
160

Costa Rica
162

Mexico
166

Cuba
180

Chocolate Cake 184   Glossary 186   Index 188

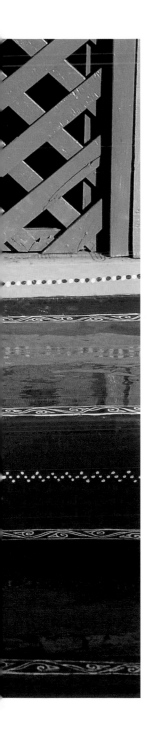

INTRODUCTION

Ten years of traveling the world in search of images and stories as a freelance photojournalist and as the Expedition Photographer-in-Residence at London's Royal Geographical Society have given me a wealth of memorable experiences. Not the least of these have involved the diverse and delicious meals I have been privileged to eat in generous people's homes and remote expedition camps, at simple street stalls and fashionable restaurants, and in dozens of countries. I started to collect recipes whenever possible, in the hope of being able to reproduce the best at home.

In 1989, I met Carolyn, already an accomplished cook, who similarly found discovering and eating exotic foods one of the greatest pleasures of travel. We began traveling together, visiting Africa, the Middle East, the Indian subcontinent, Southeast Asia, and Central and South America, accumulating ideas for globally inspired recipes with the aim of one day opening a restaurant in which we could serve all our favorite dishes from around the world. Some of the recipes we gathered from people we met along the way who were kind enough to invite us into their homes to eat or stay with them, others are traditional dishes of specific regions. Some have been worked out by observing the skills of speedy chefs in busy pavement cafés on crowded city streets, still others were patiently demonstrated by local people in jungles and deserts and on mountains — some of the world's remote places, where with so few distractions, food, especially the evening meal, is a very necessary pleasure.

As both Carolyn and I traveled as vegetarians, we were used to the challenge of finding good things to eat in places where the traditional cuisine lends itself more naturally to meat or seafood. Although this is rarely a serious problem, there have been times when we felt we were missing out on some exciting dishes simply because they were never made meatless. In such cases we adapted the traditional recipe, replacing the meat or fish with suitable alternatives to produce vegetarian versions just as tasty, with all the flavors and tastes so evocative of distant lands.

The freshly washed front doorstep of a house in Orissa in eastern India

Introduction

In 1991, we opened the World Food Café in London. The opportunity came when our friend and co-founder Nicholas Sanders offered us a 600-square-foot room on the first floor of a building he was restoring in Neal's Yard in Covent Garden. The building had previously been used as an animation studio by the Monty Python comedy team before being burnt to the ground in an accidental fire. Nicholas was in the process of rebuilding it in its original exterior style and filling it with new businesses. Our space had no plumbing, electricity, or gas — not even a floor: just four walls and three wonderful huge windows opening out on to the tree-filled peace of Neal's Yard. We wanted the café to retain this bright, open character, to provide an appealing place where we could serve meals made up from a variety of dishes from the countries we had visited. With the opportunity to design the interior from scratch, we were able to organize it so that most of the seating is around an open kitchen providing customers with a view of their food being prepared; a large table under each of the three windows enables groups of up to ten to sit together. The café is also a perfect venue to exhibit photographs taken on each trip, and to play compilations of music originating from as many countries as the food.

ABOUT THE RECIPES

The recipes in this book can all be easily cooked at home with the right ingredients; where these might be difficult to find we have suggested alternatives. Some of the dishes are those we serve every day in the World Food Café; others make only occasional appearances there. In the café, the food is usually cooked without dairy products; cheeses, yogurts, and creams are offered as optional garnishes. Meat and fish are never used. In this book, we have indicated some of the recipes that would traditionally use fish or seafood.

Spices both aromatic and hot are a common ingredient of food from the countries represented in this book. In certain extreme cases, we have eaten dishes that were distinctive for an ability to induce almost hallucinogenic states of delirium, as cocktails of pounded chilies, garlic, and ginger released their power and left mouths on fire, brows moist, and heads reeling. Any pleasure derived from this level of spicing is a very personal one, not universally shared. We have tried to achieve moderation in the use of chilies, and quantities may be

Top to bottom **Chinese characters on a red wall in Malaysia; a honey**

stall in Oaxaca, Mexico;
a dhow at sunset in
Zanzibar

reduced or increased according to taste. A number of dishes contain lots of spices other than chilies: These combine in specific amounts to form complex and unique flavors and therefore should not be altered as freely as the chili quantities. Some of the food in this book is a little more spiced than we would normally prepare it for consumption in the café, reflecting our own passion for more authentic levels of spicing.

Rice is another ingredient that requires some personal choice. Our own preference at home is to use white Indian basmati rice, which has a distinctive aroma and taste. In the café we always use brown long-grain rice, usually Italian or American, which the customers seem to prefer. Both brown and white rice work well with any of the dishes. Basmati rice does come in a brown version, and there are dozens of other types available, both brown and white, long- and short-grain, and organic — it's simply a case of choosing your favorite.

Another aspect of eating in most of the countries we have visited is the serving of several dishes at a time. In the café we have adopted this custom so that when we serve a plate of food from a particular country we include, alongside, a selection of salsas, salads, chutneys, pickles, *sambols, sambals,* dals, raitas, rice, and bread, depending on the dish's origins. Recipes for many of these accompaniments are included in the following chapters so that meals can be constructed from different combinations of them.

The book is divided geographically into four chapters and does not pretend to be a comprehensive guide to the cuisine of the regions covered, but rather reflects our personal choice of dishes enjoyed in areas we have explored. The first chapter covers Morocco and Egypt north of the Sahara, leading into Jordan and the Levant and on to Turkey and Oman; south of the Sahara we visit Mali in West Africa, then Tanzania, Kenya, and Zanzibar in East Africa, and finally the Seychelle island of La Digue in the Indian Ocean. The second chapter is dedicated to India, Nepal, and Sri Lanka. The third deals with other countries we have visited in Asia, starting with Burma, heading north to China, and then down through Southeast Asia including Laos, Thailand, Malaysia, Borneo, and Bali. In the final chapter, we take a circuitous route through the Americas, from Brazil through Bolivia, Peru, and Ecuador, then to Costa Rica and Mexico, and ending with the Caribbean island of Cuba.

The Middle East

& Africa

The Middle East & Africa

This chapter covers a vast area of the globe, from the Atlantic coast of West Africa across the continent to the Indian Ocean and over the Arabian peninsula to the shores of the Gulf. We start with Africa north of the Sahara Desert.

Morocco is a land of bountiful good food. Tagine stews — interesting concoctions of fresh vegetables, fruits, herbs, and spices — are served with hot *harissa* pastes, fluffy couscous, and nutty breads. There are thick soups and crunchy salads. And any of these may be eaten in such exotic locations as a winding medieval souk (marketplace), a fortified Atlantic port, a crumbling village in the Atlas Mountains, or a desert camp among Saharan dunes.

Farther east along the Mediterranean, in Egypt, a style of eating begins that varies little through Jordan and the Levant. There is less use of fresh vegetables and an increasing use of pulses, salads, and purées — many excellent, and most vegetarian. In fact, a traveling vegetarian can find something to eat in almost any street café from Aswan to Aleppo, the only drawback being that it will probably be the same thing in each one. Eventually, the influences of Turkey to the north or Iran to the east begin to take over.

Turkish food, like that of the Levantine countries, is often served as a *meze*, or plate, containing lots of different salads, purées, sauces, pickles, and bread, with the increased fertility of the Mediterranean's north shore providing an increasing choice of fresh vegetable ingredients.

Turkey shares with most of the Middle East a tradition of eating the very unvegetarian dish of *mensaf*, which uses a whole sheep. In the oil-rich cities of the Gulf, you are as likely to have to suffer bland fast food as *mensaf*. However, in Oman we found some very interesting dishes made in an Iranian style using rose water, nuts and dates, as well as excellent Indian curry houses catering to the migrant workers who seem to keep the country going.

In sub-Saharan Africa, despite the variety of cultures and landscapes over such a large area, the variety of cuisines can be rather limited, although there are memorable exceptions. Traveling around many of the forty or so countries between the Sahara and the Cape of Good Hope can be hard work, especially for vegetarians. Even confirmed carnivores, reduced to a diet of little more than boiled goat and cornmeal for days on end, can become desperate for a little variety. Our most memorable meals have been found in the desert fringes and delta lands of West Africa, and around the Somali coast of East Africa.

Pages 10–11 **The migration of Fulani cattle across the Niger River at Diafarabe**

Above **A bowl of succulent red olives in a Morrocan souk**

Above right **The great mud mosque at Djenné in Mali**

The cooking traditions of the Ethiopian highlands lend themselves well to vegetarian dishes, although in practice the lack of meat is more often due to economic circumstances than to personal choice. Foreign influences, such as the fiery *piri-piri* sauces of southern Africa's ex-Portuguese colonies or the rich, savory sauces of the Malay community on the South African Cape, often provide variety.

West African cooking is peppery, dominated by okra, sweet potatoes, plantain, ginger, cayenne, and peanuts. Being vegetarian there was rarely a problem, although finding anything to eat at all sometimes was. Extraordinary landscapes and friendly people are welcome distractions from hunger.

The dishes of East Africa's Somali coast and Zanzibar rely on spicy fresh-coconut-milk sauces and seafood (which may be replaced by beans and vegetables, if desired). In Ethiopia, an earthy *berberé* mixture of coarsely ground spices flavors lentil and vegetable stews eaten with wholesome breads.

Somewhere out in the Indian Ocean, between the Arabian peninsula and the coast of East Africa, a cocktail of Arab, African, Asian, and European traditions has been blended to create the Creole dishes of the Seychelles islands — providing some of the most exciting recipes in this chapter. The tiny island of La Digue where we spent our time enjoying these is the most idyllic and beautiful place we stayed in all our travels.

MOROCCO

Moroccan cooking is a blend of traditions. From the Berbers came tagines, or slow-cooked stews; *harira*, a hearty soup; and couscous, the North African staple — grains of semolina with a fine coating of wheat flour, perfectly preserved until brought to life by steam and oil, and thus ideal for long desert journeys. Bedouin Arabs introduced dried pastas, dates, and bread. More succulent additions of olives, olive oil, nuts, apricots, and herbs came from the Andalusian Moors. All this, mixed with spices from Asia, and a final French influence to give some finishing touches — such as fresh-baked baguette every morning — and Morocco couldn't go wrong. Even strict vegetarians find plenty of good things to eat, and if you don't mind a bit of lamb stock here and there it is very easy to eat in such places as the atmospheric night markets. When cooking at home, the results can be just as delicious while avoiding meat altogether.

We ate well in the markets and cafés while traveling, but the real privilege was spending time with the cooks in houses we stayed in. We were photographing beautiful houses in Marrakesh and Ouarzazate that are rented as holiday villas. Each house has a resident cook, and as we could only work in daylight we were free to spend the evenings watching and helping the cooks to prepare our evening meals, and to work out ways of keeping them meatless.

In Marrakesh, one of these houses was hidden deep in the medina, the old Arab quarter of the city. A pair of weathered wooden doors in a dusty alley opened onto a vast courtyard filled with palms, fountains, and a swimming pool and surrounded by pillared verandas shading elegant interiors. Sitting on the sumptuous cushions scattered around the flat roof, we were afforded superb views over the rooftops of the old city. One evening, the owner invited several friends to meet us, and we were soon immersed in lively conversation. Some snacks appeared from the kitchen, among them piping hot *briouats:* small pastry envelopes stuffed with a filling. They tasted good but unusual. Carolyn asked what the filling was and understood it to be Brie, which made sense as the taste was milky and the owner was French. As the evening progressed, we ate more and more of these. When we arrived for breakfast the next morning — feeling somewhat uncomfortable from the excesses of the night before — we complimented the cook on the *briouats.* She exclaimed, "Did Madame not tell you they were filled with puréed brain?" She then attempted to reassure us by saying, "Don't worry — we have not the mad cow disease here yet." This did little to stop us from feeling even more uncomfortable. All the dishes in this chapter are completely brain-free, and delicious.

An olive stall in the Marrakesh souk

MINT TEA

MAKES 6 SMALL GLASSES

2 teaspoons gunpowder green tea
    or Darjeeling
3 cups boiling water

6 sprigs mint
Sugar or honey to taste

Put the tea in a large teapot, add the boiling water and mint, and steep for about 5 minutes. Serve hot or chilled, with added sugar or honey to taste.

Mint tea is drunk in all the Moroccan pavement cafés, which are mainly frequented by men. It is unusual to see women in these places, unless they are of dubious morals. Tea is served in sturdy glasses, poured from a silver pot, and is usually very sweet. Traditionally, it is made from gunpowder green tea; we also like it with Darjeeling, as it then needs little, if any, sugar.

HARIRA SOUP

Serves 4–6

5 tablespoons olive oil

2 red onions, diced

2 garlic cloves, crushed

Handful of fresh flat-leaf parsley sprigs, chopped

1 teaspoon ground ginger

1 teaspoon coarsely ground black pepper

½ teaspoon ground saffron or turmeric

½ teaspoon cayenne pepper

1 tablespoon paprika

1 teaspoon ground coriander

2 potatoes, peeled and diced

3 carrots, peeled and diced

4 celery stalks, diced

½ cup dried green lentils

2 tablespoons tomato paste

1 pound fresh tomatoes, chopped and puréed in a food processor

2 cups vegetable stock

Water as needed

1 cup cooked chickpeas

¼ cup cooked white beans

4 ounces vermicelli, broken up

Juice of 1 lemon

Salt to taste

Heat the oil in a large, heavy saucepan over medium heat and sauté the onions and garlic until they soften.

Add the parsley, ginger, black pepper, saffron or turmeric, cayenne, paprika, and coriander, stirring to prevent sticking. Add the potatoes, carrots, celery, lentils, and tomato paste. Stir well and add the puréed tomatoes, stock, and enough water to cover all the ingredients well. Bring to a boil, reduce the heat, and simmer for 45 minutes, adding more water as necessary to make a thick soup (lentils soak up a lot of water during cooking).

Add the chickpeas, white beans, and vermicelli and cook for 5 minutes, or until the vermicelli is tender. Pour in the lemon juice and add salt.

By day, the main square in Marrakesh, the Djmaa el-Fna, is the haunt of colorful snake charmers, water sellers, and trinket sellers; as night falls, out come the storytellers, fire-eaters, acrobats, and magicians, who provide entertainment among the rows of open-air food stalls lit by blazing kerosene lanterns. Customers sit at simple wooden tables on long benches and choose portions of whatever takes their fancy from the mounds of tempting food on display.

There are lots of different recipes for *harira* soup. We ate this version as an early snack before dinner in the night market, where it is served from huge pans and eaten with wooden spoons. Some stalls sell nothing but *harira* soup, and become very busy during the Islamic fasting month of Ramadan, when a bowl of *harira* is a popular way to break the day's fast.

The atmospheric night market in Marrakesh

MARRAKESH TAGINE

SERVES 4–6

5 tablespoons olive oil

2 red onions, thinly sliced

1 level tablespoon coarsely ground black pepper

1 heaped teaspoon ground cumin

½ teaspoon ground saffron or turmeric

1 teaspoon ground cinnamon

1 small globe eggplant, cut in half lengthwise, then sliced into ½ inch half-rounds

4 small potatoes, peeled and cut into quarters

1 large sweet potato, peeled and chopped into large chunks

1 red and 1 green bell pepper, seeded, deribbed, and cut lengthwise into 1-inch-wide strips

Salt to taste

6 artichoke hearts (fresh or canned)

4 ounces green beans

4 tomatoes, peeled and coarsely chopped

1 tablespoon tomato paste

Water as needed

Handful of fresh flat-leaf parsley sprigs, chopped, plus more for garnish

Handful of fresh cilantro leaves, chopped, plus more for garnish

Small handful of raisins

Small handful of dried apricots

¼ cup pitted olives

Harissa (page 22), for serving

Crunchy baguette or couscous, for serving

Heat the oil in a large, heavy saucepan over medium heat and sauté the onions until they start to soften.

Add the spices, stirring to prevent sticking. Add the eggplant, potatoes, sweet potato, and bell peppers. Sprinkle with a little salt, as this helps to prevent the eggplant from absorbing all the oil.

When the eggplant starts to soften, add all the remaining vegetables and the tomato paste, with just enough water to barely cover the vegetables. Add the parsley, cilantro, raisins, apricots, and olives. Bring to a boil and simmer gently until all the vegetables are soft and the sauce is thick and rich, with the oil returning on the top.

Garnish with lots of parsley and cilantro, and serve with harissa and a crunchy baguette or couscous.

The Marrakesh markets are full of every imaginable herb, spice, and dried fruit, and we found that tagines tend to be much richer there than elsewhere in Morocco. We watched a sixty-year-old chef cook this tagine in the heart of the medina. Vegetables are cooked slowly and are served very soft, almost crumbling into the sauce. They are cut into large pieces to prevent them from disintegrating completely.

Marrakesh Tagine

OUARZAZATE COUSCOUS

SERVES 4–6

5 tablespoons olive oil

2 red onions, cut into 4 lengthwise wedges

Large handful of fresh flat-leaf parsley sprigs, chopped, plus more for garnish

3 tomatoes, peeled and coarsely chopped

½ teaspoon ground saffron or turmeric

1 teaspoon ground ginger

1 teaspoon ground cumin

1 teaspoon coarsely ground black pepper

1 small white cabbage (about 1 pound), cut into 6 lengthwise wedges

6 small carrots, peeled and chopped

6 small turnips, halved if large

2 cups vegetable stock

1 preserved lemon (page 22)

Water as needed

1 pound pumpkin, peeled, seeded, and cut into large cubes

6 small zucchini, partially peeled lengthwise to create a striped effect

2 cups couscous

2 cups boiling water

1 tablespoon butter

Salt to taste

1 cup toasted flaked almonds

Ground cinnamon for sprinkling

Harissa (page 22) (optional)

In a large, heavy saucepan, heat the oil over medium heat and sauté the onions until they start to soften. Add the parsley, tomatoes, and spices. Stir to avoid sticking. Add the cabbage, carrots, and turnips, and sauté to soften.

Add the stock and preserved lemon. If necessary, add water so the vegetables are nearly covered in liquid. Bring to a boil, cover, and simmer for 15 minutes. Add the pumpkin and zucchini. Simmer for another 10 to 15 minutes, until all the vegetables are very soft, adding more water if needed. The end result should be quite soupy.

While the vegetables are cooking, prepare the couscous: Place the couscous in a large bowl, add the boiling water, then let sit for 10 minutes. Fluff it with a fork or with your fingers until the grains are separated. To keep it warm, either sprinkle with water, cover, and leave in a low oven; or, if you have a steamer, steam on top of the vegetables for 10 minutes prior to serving.

We spent a few days in an amazing house overlooking a huge lake on the edge of the desert between the High Atlas and the Anti-Atlas mountains. Only a few miles along the Dades valley was an impressive collection of grand kasbahs (citadels) set among lush palm groves in the oasis of Skoura. The house was very remote, but the wonderful resident cook brought our evenings alive with nightly cookery lessons.

The food in the desert is much simpler than that found in the cities. We particularly liked a dish of vegetables cooked almost like a soup and served with lots of fluffy couscous to soak up the sauce. The vegetables were kept whole and simmered until really soft, while the couscous was steamed for two hours over a huge pot. However, we have devised a much quicker way of making it, which is given in this recipe.

The view onto the lake
at Ouarzazate

To serve, season the vegetables with salt and pour them into a colorful bowl,
or a tagine if you are lucky enough to possess one. Garnish with chopped
parsley. Stir the butter into the hot couscous, then pile on a large flat plate or
bowl. Shape into a mound and sprinkle with the toasted flaked almonds and
cinnamon. If you like spicy food, this is delicious served with Harissa (page 22)
to give it a kick.

PRESERVED LEMONS

MAKES ABOUT 1 QUART

    1 pound (4–6) lemons, plus juice of
       about 4 lemons
    ¼ cup salt

Cut the lemons into quarters and cover the cut surfaces with salt. Put the lemons in a shallow bowl and cover with a weighted plate to help release the juices. Let sit for about 30 minutes.

Put the lemons and any juices that have collected in the bowl into a hot sterilized jar, pour on the lemon juice to moisten the lemons and just cover them, then seal. Cover tightly and let sit at room temperature for about 3 weeks.

Alternatively, a quicker way is simply to cut lemons into quarters and blanch them in boiling water for 1 minute, then refresh them in cold water. This method isn't as authentic, but it allows you to have almost the real thing in minutes, and you can make just enough for Ouarzazate Couscous (page 20)!

HARISSA

MAKES ABOUT ¾ CUP

    ½ cup (2 ounces) dried hot red
       chilies
    2 tablespoons cumin seeds
    3 tablespoons coriander seeds

    4 garlic cloves
    1 teaspoon salt
    5 tablespoons olive oil

Seed and stem the chilies and soak them in warm water until soft, about 1 hour. Drain. Grind the cumin and coriander seeds finely (if you wish, you can toast them first briefly in a dry skillet for more flavor).

Put the ground spices, chilies, garlic, and salt in a food processor and process to a stiff paste. With the machine running, gradually add the olive oil until the paste becomes smooth.

A kasbah at Skoura oasis
in the Dades valley

Inset **Preserved Lemons**

Preserved lemons are an ingredient in many Moroccan dishes, and *harissa* is used as a condiment all over the Maghreb. Both are easy to make, and keep well in airtight jars in the refrigerator.

This very special, rather unusual chutney was served to us with a vegetable tagine in the heart of the medina in Marrakesh. Our hostess told us that many of her guests found it too strange, but she loved it — and so did I, although I am generally not a big fan of tomatoes.

TOMATO AND CINNAMON CHUTNEY

MAKES ABOUT ½ CUP

    5 tomatoes, chopped
    1 tablespoon packed brown sugar
    2 cinnamon sticks, ground

Combine all the ingredients in a food processor and blend until smooth. Cover amd refrigerate for at least 1 hour before serving.

CHERMOULA

Serves 4–6

5 tablespoons olive oil

2 red onions, thinly sliced

3 garlic cloves, crushed

2 teaspoons ground cumin

1 teaspoon paprika

Scant ½ teaspoon cayenne pepper

6 small potatoes, peeled and cut into quarters

1 cup water

1 pound tomatoes, chopped and puréed in a food processor

5 small zucchini, quartered lengthwise

1½ cups shelled fresh peas

1½ cups shelled fresh fava beans

Large handful of fresh cilantro leaves and stems, chopped

Juice of 1 lemon

Salt and pepper to taste

Fresh, hot baguette, for serving

Heat the oil in a large, heavy saucepan over medium heat and sauté the onions until translucent. Add the garlic and spices, stirring to keep them from sticking.

Add the potatoes and turn to coat them in the spices, then sauté for 5 minutes. Add the water and puréed tomatoes. Bring to a boil and cook briskly until the sauce has reduced to a thick, rich consistency with the oil returning on the top, adding the zucchini halfway through.

Add the peas, fava beans, and cilantro. Cover and simmer until all the vegetables are soft. You may need to add a little more water to loosen the sauce and prevent sticking.

Pour in the lemon juice and add salt and pepper. Serve with a fresh, hot baguette.

We ate this dish when our car broke down near the fishing port of Essaouira and we were waiting for the fan belt to be fixed. Everyone was incredibly helpful and we had four mechanics on the job.

Chermoula is traditionally a fish dish and always includes a mixture of cumin, paprika, cayenne, and lots of cilantro. If you eat fish, simply fry fillets of white fish until they are crunchy and add to the mixture at the end of cooking. If fresh peas and fava beans are not available, frozen are the best option.

CARROT SALAD

SERVES 4–6

12 ounces carrots

1 red onion

2 garlic cloves, crushed

2 tablespoons olive oil, plus more for sprinkling

½ teaspoon ground turmeric

½ teaspoon ground cumin

Juice of 1 lemon

Salt and pepper to taste

Lots of chopped, fresh flat-leaf parsley for garnish

Peel the carrots and slice them thickly. Cook them in salted boiling water until soft.

Meanwhile, cut the red onion in half, then slice the halves thinly. Sauté the sliced onion and garlic in the 2 tablespoons olive oil until soft. Stir in the turmeric and cumin.

Drain the carrots and plunge them into cold water. Drain again and put them in a serving bowl. Add the onion mixture, along with a good sprinkling of olive oil and the lemon juice. Season to taste and mix well.

Garnish with lots of flat-leaf parsley. Let sit for 1 hour before serving.

MOROCCAN MIXED SALAD PLATE

In Morocco, a salad of cucumber, tomato, red onion, and olives is served with almost everything, so here is a suggested mixed plate. When buying tomatoes, it is always worth choosing plump, vine-ripened beefsteak tomatoes or other large tomatoes, for the best flavor.

On a large plate, arrange slices of peeled cucumber, chunks of tomato, slices of red onion, and black and green olives. Smother them in olive oil, lemon juice, black pepper, and chopped fresh mint.

EGYPT, JORDAN & THE LEVANT

In this chapter, any of the recipes given may be eaten together in any combination: The best thing to do is to mix and match the dishes as desired, including pita bread with every meal. Bread plays an essential part in the diet of this region. Its Arabic name, *aysh*, means "life," and it is part of every meal, from the most basic street snack to the grandest Bedouin feast. All the breads of the region are unleavened; the most well known, pita, is widely available in the United States and Europe and is an ideal accompaniment to all these dishes; it is especially good for serving falafel in.

When we sailed down the Nile between Aswan and Luxor, we had to take enough food for five days. With no means of refrigeration in the scorching desert heat, our fresh supplies soon diminished, and the copious amount of fresh bread our boatman-cook had included became completely stale. However, simply by sprinkling the dry loaves with Nile water and tossing them over the coals of our fire he was able to provide us with bread that seemed as delicious as if it had just been baked — although there may well be something about cooking and eating under the stars on the bank of a great river, after a day's sailing through dramatic desert landscapes, that makes even simple food taste delicious.

In the souks of Cairo, Amman, and Damascus, we saw lavish displays of healthy vegetables piled high, but found the extent of vegetarian café food to be limited — although there were occasional surprises, such as the wonderful arugula salad encountered in Aqabah (see page 33). From Aqabah we visited Wadi Rum, where *Lawrence of Arabia* was filmed. While the desert landscape was every bit as dramatic as it had been on film, we were slightly disappointed to find coach parties arriving for "Bedu tent suppers." At Petra, however, we had no such disappointment. Riding on horseback through the narrow entrance to the gorge to come upon the majestic ruins of the ancient rose-red city was a dream achieved. We spent three days exploring Petra, the highlight of our trip to Jordan.

The last tribes of Bedouin living in the Badia Desert of eastern Jordan maintain a passion for the traditional desert style of eating mutton known as *mensaf*. This dish is a vegetarian's nightmare: A freshly slaughtered sheep is served on a bed of rice soaked in fat from the cooking; delicacies such as the tongue and eyes are offered to guests with great insistence. I spent several weeks visiting the Bedouin in their tents while photographing their way of life for the Royal Geographical Society, and when I was introduced as a vegetarian they went out of their way to provide me with alternatives.

Early-morning riders at the pyramids at Giza

The Bedouin are warm, hospitable, generous, and entertaining hosts. The harsh desert environment has inspired traditions of providing food, drink, and shelter to any passing stranger. The extreme heat of the day makes any exertion undesirable, and the shade and ventilation achieved by the design of their tents create an ideal environment in which to sit around on cushions and camel saddles escaping the unforgiving sun and indulging in long, relaxing tea-drinking ceremonies. Relatively few Bedouin still live as nomads, as falling water levels and competition for land increasingly threaten their future, and I felt very privileged to have spent some time, however brief, living among some of the last of them.

FUL MEDAMES

SERVES 4–6

3 teaspoons cumin seeds

8 tablespoons olive oil

5 garlic cloves, crushed

2 cups dried fava beans, soaked
  overnight and drained

Juice of 2 large lemons

Handful of fresh flat-leaf parsley,
  chopped, plus more to garnish

Salt and pepper to taste

Paprika, for garnish

2 lemons cut into wedges, for
  serving

Arugula and Grated Carrot Salad

2 handfuls of arugula

3 carrots, grated

Lemon juice to taste

Salt and pepper to taste

Tomato and Cucumber Salad

4 large ripe tomatoes, diced

1 large cucumber, diced

1 red onion, cut into thin slices

4 sprigs mint, chopped

Lemon juice to taste

Beet Salad

3 cooked beets, peeled and diced

1 bunch radishes, diced

2 red bell peppers, seeded,
  deribbed, and diced

Handful of fresh parsley sprigs,
  chopped

2 tablespoons olive oil

juice of 1 lemon

Toast the cumin seeds in a small skillet until they are aromatic, then grind them to a powder.

In a large saucepan, heat 3 tablespoons of the olive oil, over medium heat and sauté the garlic until soft. Add 2 teaspoons of the ground cumin and stir for a few seconds. Add the fava beans and stir until they are coated with oil.

Add enough water to cover the beans, bring to a boil, then simmer until the beans are tender, about 1 hour. You may need to add more water during this time to keep the beans moist and soupy.

Stir in the lemon juice, the remaining cumin and olive oil, the parsley, and salt and pepper. As you stir, mash the beans so they start to break down.

Pile into a large bowl and sprinkle with paprika and chopped parsley. Place lemon wedges around the edge of the bowl. Make the three salads by combining the ingredients for each, and serve with the ful medames.

Ful medames is served all across Egypt and Jordan, by everyone from street vendors and small cafés to the smartest hotels. It was our main dish on the last days of our boat journey down the Nile, and just the smell of the beans cooking brings back memories of our moonlit desert picnics.

We serve a slightly more sophisticated version of ful medames in the café, accompanied with fresh salads of beet, radishes, red onion, tomato, cucumber, carrot, plenty of parsley and cilantro leaves, and of course pita bread. Traditionally, the dish should be very garlicky and smothered in olive oil and spices. You can even serve the beans for breakfast, with fried eggs and slices of ripe tomato.

Clockwise from top left
Tabbouleh (page 31), Jordanian Arugula Salad (page 33), and Ful Medames

Above The Rose Tomb at Petra, cut out of marbled sandstone rocks

Right The entrance to the siq (gorge) at Petra, revealing the ancient pillars of the Khazneh (Treasury), one of the city's finest ruins

TABBOULEH

This is a beautiful speckled green salad from the mountains of Lebanon. We serve it with Falafel (page 32) and Hummus (page 35) or as part of a meze, a mixed salad plate.

SERVES 4–6

1 cup fine-grained cracked bulgur wheat	Juice of 2 lemons
6 tomatoes, finely diced	Salt and pepper to taste
1 small cucumber, finely diced	4 green onions, thinly sliced, for garnish
4 tablespoons olive oil	Lemon wedges, for serving

Soak the bulgur wheat in enough cold water to cover by ¼ inch and let sit for 15 minutes. The bulgur will double in size and should be light and fluffy when broken up with a fork or the fingers. If you have added too much water, pour off the excess.

Add the tomatoes, cucumber, oil, lemon juice, salt, and pepper and mix well. Garnish with green onions and serve with lemon wedges.

VARIATION

If you would like to serve tabbouleh with the less traditional dressing that we use at the World Food Café, try the recipe below.

2 teaspoons grainy mustard	Juice of 1 lemon
½ teaspoon sweet paprika	1 tablespoon cider vinegar
1 teaspoon honey	4 tablespoons olive oil

Mix the mustard, paprika, and honey until you have a smooth paste, then slowly add the lemon juice, vinegar and olive oil. Stir into the mixture of bulgur wheat, tomatoes, and cucumber.

FALAFEL

We serve these deep-fried balls of spiced mashed chickpeas in pita bread with Tabbouleh (page 31), Hummus (page 35), lettuce, and a salad of grated carrots. As the falafel are a little time-consuming to make, we advise making them in big batches and keeping them in the freezer, so they're always there and all you have to do is fry them. They also make great party food.

SERVES 4–6

2 pita breads or slices of dry bread
1 large onion, coarsely chopped
2 garlic cloves
4 teaspoons ground cumin
1 teaspoon ground pure chili
4 teaspoons flour
1 teaspoon salt
Handful of fresh flat-leaf parsley, chopped

1 cup dried chickpeas (garbanzo beans), soaked overnight and cooked until tender
Sesame seeds for coating
Oil for deep-frying, preferably sunflower

Grind the bread to crumbs in a food processor. Add the onion, garlic, cumin, chili, flour, salt, and parsley, and blend to a paste.

With the machine running, add the chickpeas and process to a thick paste. The consistency of this paste can vary slightly, depending on the moisture in the onion: If the mixture is too wet, simply make more bread crumbs and combine; if too dry, add a small amount of water while blending.

Roll the mixture between your hands into 1-inch balls and coat with sesame seeds. Fry the balls in hot oil until they are golden brown and crunchy.

If you are freezing the falafel, place plastic wrap between the layers to make them easier to separate.

Falafel are served sizzling on pavements and in street cafés everywhere. In poorer rural areas, they may share the pita with little more than some dubious-looking limp salad (best declined) and a watery tahini (a creamed sesame paste with olive oil, garlic, and lemon). In the bustling souks (markets) of Cairo, Amman, and Damascus, succulent concoctions of pickled vegetables, peppers, juicy tomatoes, crisp lettuce, yogurt, and thick creamy tahini are all crammed into the pita along with the falafel balls to provide a whole meal in the hand.

In restaurants, falafel may be served on a side plate along with assorted dips such as baba *ghanoush* (opposite) and various salads.

During a bargaining session for a Bedouin carpet in Aqabah, Jordan, we broke for lunch in a tiny backstreet café. Among other dishes, we were impressed to be served a huge plate of fresh arugula leaves with finely sliced red onion, olive oil, and lemons.

This simple yet delicious meal put us in such a good mood that we settled the carpet deal somewhat in favor of the seller. Unfortunately, the carpet's vivid colors, so exciting in the Aqabah souk, had less appeal back in London. The carpet is long since forgotten in the attic, but we still remember the arugula salad.

JORDANIAN ARUGULA SALAD

SERVES 4–6

3 large handfuls arugula

Handful of unstemmed fresh flat-leaf parsley sprigs

4 tomatoes, diced

2 red onions, cut in half then thinly sliced

1 bunch radishes, sliced

2 tablespoons olive oil

Juice of ½ lemon

Pinch of ground cumin

Salt and pepper to taste

Mix the arugula and parsley. Make a bed of this in a salad bowl. On top of it, pile the tomato, onion and radishes.

Make a dressing with the olive oil, lemon juice, cumin, salt, and pepper. Pour this over the salad and serve immediately.

BABA GHANOUSH

This eggplant dip is good served with warm pita bread.

SERVES 4–6

1 large eggplant

2 garlic cloves

2 tablespoons tahini

1 tablespoon olive oil

Salt and pepper to taste

Juice of 1 lemon

Chopped fresh flat-leaf parsley, for garnish

Paprika, for garnish

Grill the eggplant until the skin starts to bubble, turning it regularly until all sides are browned and the eggplant feels soft. (This can also be done in a preheated 400°F oven.)

Halve the eggplant and scoop out the flesh into a food processor. Add the garlic, tahini, olive oil, salt, pepper, and lemon juice, then blend until smooth.

Pile on a flat plate, garnish with parsley, and sprinkle with paprika.

LENTIL SOUP

SERVES 4–6

1¾ cups red lentils

3 tablespoons olive oil

2 large onions, finely chopped

3 garlic cloves, crushed

4 cups vegetable stock

1½ teaspoons cumin seeds

1½ teaspoons red pepper flakes

Salt and freshly ground black pepper
to taste

Juice of 1 lemon

Handful of fresh flat-leaf parsley
sprigs, chopped

Rinse the lentils until the water runs clear. Heat the oil in a large, heavy saucepan over medium heat and sauté the onions until soft. Add the garlic and sauté for a few seconds.

Add the lentils to the pan and stir well until coated with oil. Add the stock and bring to a boil. If foam rises to the top, scoop off and discard.

Toast the cumin seeds in a dry skillet until aromatic, then grind to a powder. Add this to the soup with the pepper flakes. Cover and simmer until the lentils are really soft and start to break down. You may need to add water during this time, as lentils absorb a lot of liquid during cooking.

Add salt, black pepper, and lemon juice. Blend in a processor until smooth. Garnish with lots of parsley.

WHITE BEAN SALAD

SERVES 4–6

One 15-ounce can butter beans,
drained

6 green onions, sliced

2 garlic cloves, crushed

2 tomatoes, diced

4 sprigs mint, chopped

1 small cucumber, peeled and finely
diced

1 green bell pepper, seeded,
deribbed, and finely diced

Handful of fresh flat-leaf parsley
sprigs, chopped

Salt and pepper to taste

Juice of 1 lemon

2 tablespoons olive oil

Black olives, for garnish

Combine all the ingredients except the black olives. Garnish with the olives and serve.

The lips of a statue at Luxor dating from 4,000 years ago

HUMMUS

Serves 4–6

1 cup dried chickpeas (garbanzo
    beans), soaked overnight in
    plenty of water
2 garlic cloves
Juice of 1½ lemons

3 tablespoons olive oil, plus more
    for drizzling
3 tablespoons tahini
Ground cumin, to garnish

Drain the chickpeas and cook them in plenty of simmering water until tender. Squash one between your fingers to see if they are done. Drain and let cool. Put the chickpeas, garlic, lemon juice, oil, and tahini in a food processor and blend until a thick paste forms. Add a little water, bit by bit, until the hummus becomes smooth and creamy. Season with salt. Turn out into a bowl and sprinkle with cumin, then drizzle with olive oil.

TURKEY

Despite the extent and centuries-long duration of the Ottoman Empire, the Turks did not trade extensively with other nations or really receive an influx of foreign populations or cuisines. However, Turkish cooking uses many ingredients common also to the cuisines of Greece to the west and the Arab countries to the southeast.

One of our favorite meals in Turkey is breakfast. Warm, fresh bread with local honey and butter, salty black olives, white sheep's-milk cheese, and lots of refreshing tea is the standard hotel breakfast from Istanbul to the seaside villages of the Aegean. I ate my most memorable breakfast one day when I was the only passenger out on the deck of a ferry on a winter crossing of the Sea of Marmara. It was a bitterly cold morning, but the sight of the mosques of Istanbul appearing in the distance through the sea mist was well worth braving the cold for — especially as breakfast was served with a winter specialty of hot sweetened milk flavored with orchidroot, and cinnamon.

Chilies and lemons hanging up for sale on the Mediterranean coast of Turkey

IMAM'S EGGPLANT

SERVES 4–6

5 tablespoons olive oil

2 globe eggplants, diced

Salt to taste

3 cups shredded cabbage, sliced

2 teaspoons paprika

1¼ cups (14 ounces) tomato purée
    or 6 tomatoes, puréed

Water as needed

Large handful of fresh flat-leaf
    parsley sprigs, chopped

6 sprigs mint, minced

Juice of 1 lemon

1 tablespoon honey or packed
    brown sugar

Pepper to taste

The main component of the Turkish *meze* (mixed plate) that we serve in the World Food Café is this dish of eggplant and cabbage cooked in an herb and tomato sauce. We have come across similar dishes in Greek and Syrian cooking, usually known as "the imam swooned," after a tale of an imam (Muslim prayer leader) who was so impressed with the taste that he fainted. We're not sure where the story or the recipe is originally from, so as we ate it first in Turkey we have included it here.

The rest of our *mezes* were collected from all over the Middle East, including a mashed carrot salad, a tabbouleh, a hummus, and olives.

Heat the oil in a large saucepan, over medium heat. Add the eggplant and sprinkle it with a little salt to prevent it from absorbing all the oil and drying out. Sauté the eggplant until it starts to soften, then add the cabbage. Continue sautéing until both vegetables are soft. Add the paprika and stir until the vegetables are coated. Add the tomato purée and a little water to make a sauce. Bring to a boil, reduce heat, and simmer until thickened and rich. You may need to add a little more water to prevent sticking.

Add the parsley, mint, lemon juice, honey or sugar, pepper and salt to taste. Cook for 5 minutes to allow all the flavors to combine.

Serve with Mashed Carrot Salad (page 39), black olives, yogurt and cucumber, and pita bread, or with Tabbouleh (page 31) and Hummus (page 35).

TOMATO, CUCUMBER, AND GREEN PEPPER

This works well in any Turkish meze. We ate it for breakfast, lunch, and dinner.

SERVES 4–6

4 ripe tomatoes, diced

1 cucumber, diced

2 green bell peppers, seeded,
    deribbed, and diced

Olive oil to taste

Pepper to taste

Simply combine all the ingredients.

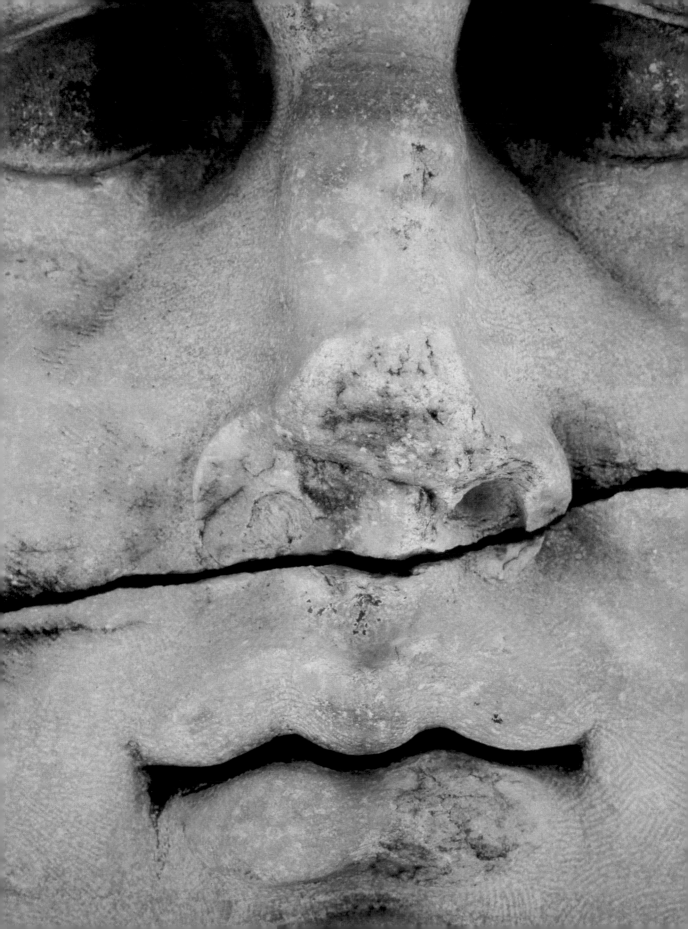

MASHED CARROT SALAD

This recipe is also delicious with yogurt stirred into it.

SERVES 4–6

1 pound carrots, peeled and sliced

Salt to taste

2 teaspoons cumin seeds

Juice of 1 lemon

3 tablespoons olive oil

1 teaspoon ground black pepper

2 teaspoons sweet paprika

Cook the carrots in salted boiling water until tender. Drain and place in a large bowl, then mash with a potato masher until smooth.

Toast the cumin seeds in a small skillet, then grind to a powder. Add to the mashed carrot with the remaining ingredients and mix well.

YOGURT WITH CUCUMBER

This makes a very popular side dish with any meal.

SERVES 4–6

1 cucumber, peeled and finely diced

1 cup plain yogurt, preferably
  sheep's milk

4 sprigs mint, chopped

Salt and pepper to taste

1 tablespoon olive oil

In a bowl, combine all the ingredients except the olive oil. Just before serving, pour the oil over the top of the salad.

A detail of the cracked face of a statue in the ruins at Didyma, an ancient sanctuary and oracle of Apollo

The Middle East & Africa

OMAN

In Oman, where meat is the customary offering to guests, the most interesting regional vegetarian dishes we found were in roadhouse truck stops on the desert highway that stretches for hundreds of miles across the "empty quarter," linking the capital, Muscat, with Salalah, capital of the southern Dhofar region. These highway rest stops are typical of the extreme contrasts in Oman. They are as clean and modern as if they were in Muscat, yet located in the heart of one of the most rugged and empty parts of the globe. Just inland from the gleaming high-tech cityscapes of Muscat, the Jebel Akhdar is a mountainous region of dirt roads and ancient villages, inhabited by turbaned men and veiled women. Age-old traditions of hospitality are still observed, and we often found ourselves guests in people's homes, consuming dates and cardamom coffee.

Salalah is in many ways the most modern city in Oman; investment has been encouraged by the government. It is also a historic center of the frankincense trade, on the edge of Dhofar, a wild land of warring tribes, remote mosques, and desolate coastline. One fairly new development has been the establishment of a dairy industry, and in pastures recalling rural England, imported Friesian cattle graze alongside camels nibbling frankincense trees — another of the wonderful juxtapositions of modern Oman.

It may have been partly our relief at finding civilization in the wilderness, or perhaps the temptation of an unlimited buffet, but one way or another gluttony was an easy sin at the highway rest stops in Oman. Bowls of eggplant in puréed date and yogurt sauce, and mounds of rose water rice are two of the delicious vegetarian dishes we found.

ROSE WATER RICE

SERVES 4–6

2 tablespoons butter
½ cup pistachios
1 cup almonds
⅔ cup seedless raisins
¼ cup dried apricots, quartered
2 cups long-grain white rice

½ teaspoon ground cardamom
4 teaspoons rose water
Grated zest of 1 orange, preferably organic

Melt the butter in a large pan over medium heat and fry the nuts until brown. Add the raisins and apricots. Set aside and keep warm.

Cook the rice in a large pan of simmering salted water until it is just tender. Drain well and sprinkle with the cardamom.

Add the nuts and fruit, sprinkle with rose water and orange zest, and serve.

The Jebel Akhdar
Mountains

EGGPLANT IN DATE SAUCE

SERVES 4–6

4 tablespoons oil

3 red onions, thinly sliced

1 small globe eggplant (1 pound), cubed

Salt to taste

1 teaspoon ground cinnamon

½ teaspoon ground ginger

¼ teaspoon ground allspice

1 cup vegetable stock

¼ cup dates, pitted

Juice of 1 lemon

1 tablespoon rose water

Water as needed

In a large skillet, heat the oil over medium heat and sauté the onions until they are soft. Add the eggplant and sprinkle it with a little salt to prevent it from absorbing all the oil and drying out. Sauté, stirring constantly, until the eggplant is browned. Add the spices and sauté for 1 minute. Add the stock and simmer slowly for about 10 minutes. In a food processor, purée the dates with the lemon juice and rose water, adding enough water to make a creamy paste. Add this paste to the eggplant, stir in, and serve.

MALI

The countries of French-speaking West Africa have inherited many food customs from their colonial past. Croissants, baguettes, and café au lait are ubiquitous in restaurants and cafés — even in Bamako, capital of Mali, one of West Africa's poorest and least developed states. However, the street food, cooked and served outdoors, belongs to quite another tradition: The ingredients and style are wholly African.

The highlight of our trip to Mali was the annual migration of Fulani cattle across the Niger at the island village of Diafarabe (pages 10–11). Getting there took days of hard travel. We arrived at night to find a crowded village with no electricity. Dawn revealed mud houses and a mosque among palm trees; fishermen casting nets into the Niger; and hundreds of cooking fires filling the air with the smells of African breakfasts. The herdsmen and cattle had been away in the Sahel for months, and their return was cause for celebration. Wives and families gathered on the riverbank dressed in all their finery, as the Fulani chiefs, mounted on decorated horses and camels, galloped out of the desert in clouds of dust, then rode through the river, followed by thousands of cattle. The crossing continued long into the night, by which time Diafarabe was alive with music, amplified with megaphones powered by truck batteries, and dancing lit by hand torches.

WEST AFRICAN BEANS AND OKRA

SERVES 4–6

4 tablespoons oil	10 ounces green beans
1 onion, puréed	Handful of fresh cilantro leaves,
1 teaspoon cayenne pepper	chopped
1 tablespoon fresh thyme, chopped	2 cups cooked black-eyed peas
18 okra pods, cut in half lengthwise	Salt and pepper to taste
4 tomatoes, chopped and puréed in	Water as needed
a food processor	

Heat the oil in a large saucepan over medium heat and sauté the onion until soft. Add the cayenne and thyme and cook briefly. Add the okra, tomatoes, green beans, and cilantro, and cook over low heat for 15 minutes, stirring occasionally. Add the black-eyed beans, mashing them a little with a fork. Season with salt and pepper and add a little water to loosen the mixture. Serve.

This is a typical West African dish using okra, one of the most common vegetables of the region. We ate it at the weekly market in Djenné, near the mighty 15th-century mud-built mosque (page 13). The market brought to life the dusty square in front of the mosque and the sleepy alleys; people poured in from the countryside, and food stalls appeared all around the square.

Jollof is a style of eating rice that usually includes meat and makes a meal in itself. This recipe is designed to cook rice in a similar way, but without meat. It makes a good accompaniment to the bean and okra dish opposite, or to Sweet Potatoes in a Cayenne, Ginger, and Peanut Sauce (page 44).

Pirogues — traditional canoes — on the Niger River

WEST AFRICAN JOLLOF RICE

SERVES 4–6

3 tablespoons butter

2 large onions, thinly sliced

2 large green bell peppers, seeded, deribbed, and diced

1 teaspoon cayenne pepper

1 teaspoon ground black pepper

½ teaspoon ground allspice

8 ounces tomatoes, finely chopped

½ cup tomato purée

1 tablespoon chopped fresh thyme

2 cups rice, rinsed

Water as needed

Salt to taste

Melt the butter in a large saucepan over medium heat. Add the onions, peppers, and spices, increase the heat, and sauté for 1 minute. Add the tomatoes and sauté for 1 minute. Stir in the tomato purée and thyme and sauté for 1 more minute. Add the rice, mix well, and cover with water. Cover and bring to a boil. Reduce heat and simmer until the water is absorbed, about 15 minutes. Season with salt and serve.

SWEET POTATOES IN A CAYENNE, GINGER, AND PEANUT SAUCE

SERVES 4–6

4 tablespoons sunflower oil

1 large onion, cubed

4 garlic cloves, crushed

2-inch piece fresh ginger, peeled and minced

1¾ pounds sweet potatoes, peeled and cubed

1 pound white cabbage, cubed

2 teaspoons paprika

1 teaspoon cayenne pepper

1¾ cups (14 ounces) chopped plum tomatoes

1 cup pineapple juice

½ cup smooth peanut butter

Salt and pepper to taste

Garnish

2 carrots, peeled and grated

2 beets, peeled and grated

2 bananas, peeled and sliced

Juice of 1 lime

Handful of fresh cilantro leaves, chopped

Heat the sunflower oil in a large, heavy pan over medium heat and sauté the onion until soft. Add the garlic and ginger, sauté for a few minutes, then add the sweet potatoes and cabbage.

When the vegetables start to soften, add the paprika and cayenne. Stir to coat the vegetables with the spices. Add the chopped tomatoes and pineapple juice. Cover the pan and simmer until the vegetables are soft.

Stir in the peanut butter until well combined. Add salt and pepper.

Toss the carrots, beets, and bananas in the lime juice and sprinkle over the dish, together with the cilantro. Serve with rice.

This spicy sweet potato recipe is our all-time favorite West African dish, and one of our best memories of Mali. We tasted it on a riverboat journey along the Niger. Rather than eat the foul meals in the ship's restaurant, several Malians came equipped with stoves, pots, and hampers of ingredients, and subsidized their fares by selling hearty stews.

We serve our version every day in the World Food Café. Each time we try to take it off the menu we are obliged by popular demand to bring it back. The ground peanuts make a creamy sauce, enlivened with the fresh ginger, garlic, and cayenne.

Sweet Potatoes in a Cayenne, Ginger, and Peanut Sauce

EAST AFRICA

East Africa is no paradise for vegetarians. Except in the Indian curry houses of the cities, meat or seafood dishes are the most likely choice in any café or street stall anywhere in Kenya or Tanzania. However, the spectacular skies, dramatic landscapes, wild animals, and beautiful coastlines help to compensate for the lack of good vegetarian food. The most interesting dishes we found were on the Kenyan island of Lamu and the Tanzanian island of Zanzibar.

    Apart from Zanzibar, my main experience of Tanzania was photographing a Royal Geographical Society project in the heart of the savannah lands of the Mkomazi Game Reserve. The reserve had never been developed or promoted as an international

A Masai tribesman on the edge of the Rift Valley in Tanzania

attraction, and the scientists were living in a group of huts on an escarpment over-looking the grasslands and the Paree Mountains beyond, in the middle of an undisturbed wilderness. On arrival, I was allocated a Land Rover and a ranger with a gun, and was given the freedom of the reserve. This turned out to be a dream assignment, giving me unlimited opportunity to photograph the African bush and enjoy some thrilling encounters with truly wild animals.

My next job was to photograph a luxury safari in the Serengeti and Ngorongoro Crater parks, including dawn balloon rides, lavish catering, and five-star accommodations. Having previously imagined that *this* would be the dream assignment, in practice I found the experience of being driven around the bush with a group much less exciting than that of being out on my own.

ZANZIBAR BEANS IN COCONUT SAUCE

For a more authentic version of this dish, fresh fish or seafood can be used instead of the sweet potatoes.

SERVES 4–6

Zanzibar, politically part of Tanzania, owes its cooking traditions more to Arab and European colonialism and to Indian traders than to mainland East Africa. Coconut-palm groves and spice plantations provide ingredients for tasty sauces.

We rented a house with a cook on the quiet east coast. He was most enthusiastic about cooking us lobster, giant prawns, and fish fillets in a rich coconut-cream sauce, but we managed to get him to prepare the same sauce with beans and fried sweet potatoes, as given here, and it was just as good.

6 tablespoons oil	4 cardamom pods, split
1 pound sweet potatoes, peeled and cut into ¾-inch cubes	2 teaspoons ground turmeric
1 large onion, finely chopped	6 green Thai or serrano chilies, cut into quarters lengthwise
6 garlic cloves, crushed	Handful of fresh cilantro leaves
2-inch piece fresh ginger, peeled and minced	14 ounces canned coconut milk
4 black peppercorns, coarsely ground	2 cups cooked pinto beans or black-eyed peas
6 cloves, coarsely ground	Salt to taste

Heat half the oil in a heavy saucepan over medium heat and fry the sweet potato until almost cooked through. Set aside.

In the remaining oil, sauté the onion, garlic, and ginger until soft. Add all the spices with the chilies and cilantro, and cook, stirring, for 3 minutes.

Add the coconut milk, sweet potatoes, and beans. Simmer gently until the sweet potatoes are quite tender. Season with salt and serve.

BERBERÉ PASTE

In Ethiopia, berberé *means red chili powder, but it is also the spicy paste that makes Ethiopian food so distinctive. It can be made in advance and kept in the fridge for up to 6 weeks.*

SERVES 4–6

2 garlic cloves

½-inch piece fresh ginger, peeled and coarsely chopped

3 green onions, sliced

1 tablespoon cider vinegar

½ teaspoon black peppercorns

½ teaspoon cardamom seeds

½ teaspoon coriander seeds

½ teaspoon fenugreek seeds

4 cloves

1 teaspoon cumin seeds

7 small, dried red peppers

¼ teaspoon ground cinnamon

¼ teaspoon ground nutmeg

1 teaspoon salt

4 teaspoons ground paprika

¼ teaspoon ground allspice

In a food processor, blend the garlic, ginger, onions, and vinegar until a paste forms.

Toast the peppercorns, cardamom seeds, coriander seeds, fenugreek seeds, cloves, and cumin seeds in a hot skillet until fragrant. Add the peppers and grind the mixture finely in a spice grinder or using a pestle and mortar. Add to the paste.

Add all the remaining ingredients and mix well. Store in a well-sealed container.

Ethiopia, in northern East Africa, can be a schizophrenic country for a vegetarian traveler. Ethiopians have a unique and interesting tradition of spicy stews, or *wats* (*w'ets*), based on lamb, goat, or beef. However, many Ethiopians are Orthodox Christians required to "fast" on Wednesdays and Fridays. "Fasting" in this sense consists of eating *wats* without the meat — so you can find many tasty Ethiopian *wats* made using vegetables, beans, and lentils. During Lent in March and April, there are several weeks of fasting, when vegetarians can feast daily without restriction.

The two recipes given here are for *berberé* paste — essential to a good *wat* — and a *wat* made with mixed vegetables.

ETHIOPIAN VEGETABLE WAT

Any combination of vegetables can be used in this dish; the mixture used here is just a suggestion. In Ethiopia, the traditional accompaniment to this wat *would be* injera, *a spongy, slightly fermented flat bread. In the café, we serve it with cheese-and-herb bread, cottage cheese, and salad.*

SERVES 4–6

3 tablespoons butter

1 large onion, thinly sliced

2 garlic cloves, crushed

1 tablespoon berberé paste (see opposite)

1 teaspoon paprika

1 teaspoon ground turmeric

1 teaspoon ground cardamom seeds

Pinch of ground clove

3-inch piece cinnamon stick, ground

3 carrots, peeled and cubed

3 potatoes, cubed

3 zucchini, chopped into chunks

7 ounces green beans, chopped

7 ounces baby spinach leaves, chopped

14 ounces canned chopped tomatoes

1 cup vegetable stock

Salt and pepper to taste

6 fresh basil leaves, torn up

Handful of fresh cilantro leaves, chopped

Melt the butter in a large, heavy saucepan over medium heat and sauté the onion, garlic, and berberé paste for 3 minutes. Add the spices and cook, stirring, for 2 minutes more. Add all the fresh vegetables and stir into the spices. Continue to cook for 10 minutes, stirring occasionally.

Add the tomatoes with their liquid and the stock, bring to a boil, reduce heat, and simmer until the vegetables are all cooked, adding more water if needed. Season with salt and pepper.

Finally, add the torn basil leaves and cilantro.

MKOMAZI CARDAMOM-MASHED SWEET POTATOES WITH PEPPER RELISH

This dish, served here with a zingy relish, would also be good with an onion sauce.

SERVES 4–6

Pepper Relish

3 garlic cloves

3 fresh red Thai or serrano chilies

4 tomatoes, chopped

1 onion, chopped

1 large red bell pepper, seeded, deribbed, and chopped

Handful of fresh parsley sprigs, stemmed

Juice of 1 lemon

Salt and pepper to taste

1 sweet potatoes (8 ounces) peeled and sliced

1½ cups corn kernels

1 cup shelled fresh peas

1 small bunch spinach, stemmed and chopped

3 tablespoons butter

1 large onion, sliced

1 teaspoon ground cardamom

Salt and pepper to taste

1 teaspoon honey

Well ahead, make the relish: In a food processor, blend together all the ingredients. Set aside, preferably in the fridge, and let sit as long as you can – the longer the better.

Cook the sweet potato in salted boiling water until tender. Drain.

Cook the corn and peas in salted boiling water until tender. Just before the end of cooking, add the spinach to wilt it briefly. Drain.

Melt the butter in a heavy saucepan over medium heat and fry the onion until it is well caramelized.

Combine the sweet potato and onion, sprinkle with the cardamom, salt, and pepper. Mash, adding more butter if desired. Add the other vegetables and mix in the honey.

Serve hot, with the relish and a green salad.

During my stay on the Mkomazi Game Reserve in Tanzania, the camp cook noticed my lack of enthusiasm for his meat stews and offered to cook me something special if I drove him to the village for some ingredients. Gathering the ingredients took about half an hour; sitting around in the bar meeting all his friends over several beers took the rest of the afternoon.

After weeks of meat stews, the others in the camp were so interested in my superb meal that the cook found himself making it for everyone the following evening.

Mkomazi Cardamom-Mashed Sweet Potatoes with (inset) Pepper Relish

CASSAVA AND CELERY IN MUNG DAL GRAVY

We were served this dish in a Nairobi home as a vegetarian alternative to the traditional meat sauces that accompany the cornmeal staple ugali. We serve it with rice and salad instead of ugali. Cassava is not always easy to find (sometimes it is available frozen) and must be well cooked. Sweet potatoes make a perfectly acceptable alternative.

SERVES 4–6

1¼ cups mung dal (yellow split peas)

1½ pounds cassava or sweet potatoes, peeled and cut into ¾-inch dice

4 tablespoons peanut oil

2 large onions, finely chopped

1 teaspoon ground turmeric

1 teaspoon chili powder

1 teaspoon paprika

1 head celery, chopped small

Salt to taste

Water as needed

Cook the mung dal in boiling water until tender. Drain and partially mash. Blanch the cassava or sweet potatoes in salted boiling water for about 10 minutes. Drain and set aside.

Heat the oil in a large, heavy pan over medium heat and sauté the onions until they are soft. Add the spices and sauté 1 minute more. Add the cassava and celery. Sauté until the vegetables are tender, 2–3 minutes.

Stir in the cooked dal, salt, and enough water to give a saucelike consistency.

Orphaned baby elephants in the Daphne Scheldrick Sanctuary of Nairobi Park

THE SEYCHELLES: LA DIGUE ISLAND

La Digue is one of the 115 islands of the Seychelles. With a population of around 2,000, it is a friendly and relaxed place, with all the trappings of a tropical paradise. There are abundant forests full of fruits; palm-fringed beaches of white sand, and warm, clear water full of fish; and long days of sunshine and blue sky. We also discovered some wonderful food.

We stayed in an old French colonial plantation house converted into a guest house, where the evening meals provided by the family that own and run it were exceptional. The cooks were more than happy to let us sit in on their preparations and see how they created the meals we were eating. The recipes we give in this chapter are two of our favorites.

La Digue was an uninhabited desert island until just over 200 years ago. It was first settled by French colonialists and their slaves, then gained by the British, along with most of the Indian Ocean islands, as spoils of the Napoleonic wars. With the abolition of slavery, the British encouraged the migration of Indians and Asians to the islands. La Digue gradually developed as a community with the rich ethnic blend of African, Asian, Arab, and European roots and cultural influences that define the Creole-speaking Seychellois and their food. The finest traditional cooking is probably found in the guest houses, where meals are eaten communally as buffet feasts. Fresh fish and Creole sauces dominate, and there are also some delicious and inventive vegetable and salad accompaniments.

Much of the appeal of La Digue lies in the things it lacks — such as tropical diseases, crime, cars, poverty, pollution, large hotels, crowds, and dangerous wildlife. Being such an intimate island society, violent crime is virtually unheard of, and even petty theft is extremely rare. Apart from the island's two taxis, vehicles are restricted to a few pickups, used by the local farmers and traders; bicycles; and creaking oxcarts — which also operate as taxis.

The island is only 2½ miles long, and cycling is a pleasure on the shaded, carless roads that give access to most of the coast and the less mountainous parts of the interior. If you leave your bike, unlocked, at the end of a road and continue by foot, jungly tracks will take you to some of the most stunning beaches in the world.

One of the paradise beaches of La Digue island

In the Seychelles, Sweet Apple Salad is almost always served with Creole dishes. Golden apples — tart green apples rather like small Granny Smiths, but with flesh that is drier and more yellow — are combined with *bredes*, a local variety of spinach that is in fact more like napa cabbage. The resulting salad is a wonderful balance of sweet, savory, and spicy.

SWEET APPLE SALAD

SERVES 4–6

4 tart apples, peeled, cored, and grated

4 cups thinly sliced napa cabbage

2 tablespoons sunflower oil

1 large red onion, halved and thinly sliced

2 green Thai or serrano chilies, thinly sliced

½ teaspoon ground turmeric

1-inch piece fresh ginger, grated

Juice of 2 limes

Pepper and salt to taste

Combine the grated apple and sliced cabbage. Heat the oil in a skillet over medium heat and sauté the onion until it starts to soften. Add the chilies, turmeric, and ginger and sauté for a further 30 seconds.

Stir the contents of the pan into the salad, then sprinkle with the lime juice and pepper. Add salt to taste and mix well.

Chill for 30 minutes before serving.

CARRI COCO CURRY

SERVES 4–6

Curry Mixture
10 curry leaves
1 teaspoon ground cinnamon
½ teaspoon chili powder
1 teaspoon ground allspice
¼ teaspoon cayenne pepper
1 teaspoon ground black pepper
1 teaspoon ground turmeric

½ cup (1 stick) butter
1 tablespoon sunflower oil
2 large onions, diced
5 garlic cloves, crushed
1½-inch piece fresh ginger, peeled
  and grated
2 sweet potatoes (preferably orange-
  fleshed), peeled and cut into
  cubes

4 carrots (about 1 pound), peeled
  and cubed
1 piece butternut squash, peeled,
  seeded, and cubed
Water as needed
1 pound napa cabbage, cut into
  1-inch strips
Large handful of fresh flat-leaf
  parsley sprigs, minced
Leaves from small handful of thyme,
  minced
1¼ cups coconut milk
Salt and pepper to taste

Garnish
2 plantains, peeled
2 tablespoons oil or butter
Salt to taste

Combine all the curry mixture ingredients. Melt the butter with the oil in a large saucepan over medium heat. Sauté the onions, garlic, and ginger until tender. Add the curry mixture and stir.

Add the sweet potatoes, carrots, and squash. Stir until the vegetables are well coated with spice mix. Add just enough water to barely cover the vegetables. Bring to a boil, reduce heat to low and simmer until the vegetables just start to soften.

Add the cabbage, parsley, thyme, and coconut milk. Cook gently for 10 minutes, making sure the coconut milk does not boil. Season with salt and pepper.

While the curry is cooking, slice the plantain and sauté the slices in hot oil or butter until crunchy on the outside and soft inside. Sprinkle with salt.

Serve with rice, fried plantain slices, and Sweet Apple Salad (page 55).

Coco curry is traditionally made with coconut milk and herbs, and served with fish. Sweet potato, cassava, and breadfruit form a large part of the Creole daily diet, so those are what we cook it with at the World Food Café. You can, however, make it with almost any vegetable. We have chosen sweet potato and butternut squash, which are more readily available.

Sweet Apple Salad (front) and Carri Coco Curry (back)

India, Nepal &

Sri Lanka

India, Nepal & Sri Lanka

A plate of several Indian dishes, called a *thali*, is a daily feature of the World Food Café menu. The many regional variations of Indian cooking provide a wide choice of cooking styles for the main dish, which is served with homemade chutneys, salads, raitas, and rice. Indian cuisine displays an extensive range of vegetarian cooking, and the friendly hospitality of the people, their love of food, and their eagerness to share how it is prepared have given us a great collection of recipes. Some of these we gathered without a word of common language in remote rural homes; others were demonstrated in fluent English in smart city apartments; still others were acquired in quite bizarre circumstances.

Traveling in India can be a confusing mix of sensuous experiences. During one trip there, I read in a book the line "like mustard gas and roses." The phrase, for me, sums up traveling in India. Smells as gross as mustard gas and as sweet as roses come within seconds of each other. Sights are seductive, poetic, and romantic as often as they are revolting, pitiful, and disturbing. Travel can include many hours of boredom, discomfort, and frustration and just as many of excitement, luxury, and pleasure. Traveling anywhere has elements of all these aspects, but India manages to deliver more of them, more often, and more extremely.

All the domestic airlines have vegetarian food on board, while long rail journeys are made even more memorable by excellent vegetarian *thalis* delivered freshly cooked to your seat. Roadside cafes, or *dhabas*, where the long-distance buses stop, provide quick feasts for hundreds at a time. If you travel by hired car, you will inevitably have a driver who knows the best *dhabas* and will be pleased to stop when you fancy a roadside meal. Some hotels have good buffets with many vegetarian options, although often a better meal can be found for a modest sum in a local café. There is no shortage of interesting vegetarian street food: On city streets, railway platforms, and beaches, at bus stations, markets, and even lonely road junctions, there are stalls churning out sizzling snacks.

We have divided India into north, east, south, and west to reflect the areas where we discovered different dishes. There are far more complex regional variations than this in Indian cooking, and the mobility of the population means you can end up eating almost anything, anywhere. In general, the food of the south often includes coconut and is served with lots of rice, pickles, chutneys, and small side dishes. In the north, there is a fondness for ghee (clarified butter) and paneer (fried cheese); the food can be rich and oily and is often served with bread to

Above **A snack seller in southern India displays his enticing wares**

Right **Children in the Shekhawati district of Rajasthan; the pleasure of travel in India has as much to do with the beauty and sense of humor of the people as it does with the seductive landscapes.**

Pages 58–59 **Crossing the bridge, Madurai, Tamil Nudu**

soak up the oil. Some dishes, such as *aloo gobi*, turn up all over India in various styles. In poorer rural areas, the options may be as limited as dal, rice, and samosas, while in cities the choice can be bewildering. Nepal and Sri Lanka, both bordering India although thousands of miles apart, have cuisines influenced by the style of Indian cooking. Meals in Nepal are usually robust and filling combinations of boiled rice, creamy dal, and spiced vegetables, providing good fuel for long walks between mountain villages. The year-round tropical heat of Sri Lanka encourages lighter meals, with an emphasis on coconuts, curry leaves, and tangy mixtures of fresh fruit and fiery chilies.

In the World Food Café, we serve the Indian *thali* with long-grain brown rice. The amount of chili to use is a personal decision; these recipes use the amount shown to us by the people who made the dishes. In the café, we advise those sensitive to spicy food to avoid the Indian dishes, but most customers find them fine. If you reduce the quantity of chili in any recipe you won't alter the overall flavor too much, so feel free to scale the heat down (or up) as you prefer.

NORTHERN INDIA

The far north of India has more in common with Tibet than it does with the rest of the subcontinent. The Himalayan peaks and snowfields of Ladakh form a backdrop to Buddhist monasteries and shrines; most of the people are Tibetan rather than Indian in origin, a fact reflected in the style of the food. The lake district of Kashmir is distinctive in a different way, owing more to the Islamic traditions of Central Asia than to the plains of India. Kashmiri-inspired dishes crop up all over the north. Sadly, since our last visit at the end of the 1980s, Kashmir has effectively been closed to casual tourism. We still have fond memories of home-cooked meals eaten on wooden houseboats on Dal Lake.

Water taxis like this elegant yellow *shikara* are used to ferry tourists and Kashmiris around Dal and Naki lakes

Dal and rice form the staple diet across India. The recipe for fried dal given here is less refined than some in this chapter, yet the dish is utterly delicious.

Located in the foothills of the Himalayas along the floodplain of the Ramganga River, the Corbet National Park is only few hours north of Delhi, yet it could not be a more serene and peaceful place. The first time we went there, we had unrealistic expectations of seeing a wild tiger. The dawn and dusk elephant rides through the forest, the sightings of deer, monkeys, and other wildlife, the great natural beauty, and the fine evening meals in the forest lodge were all very enjoyable, but we still felt frustrated by the lack of tiger. When we left I filled in the visitors' book and was asked to list all the animals I had seen. I cheekily ended by writing "BUT NO TIGER" — and was left feeling slightly ridiculous when the bus to the park gates had to stop to wait for a fine, full-grown tigress and her cubs to stroll across the road and off into the jungle.

FRIED DAL

Split peas are cooked until they form a creamy soup; the spices are fried and added at the end of the cooking. Serve the dal with rice or as an accompaniment to any curry.

SERVES 4–6

1¼ cups yellow split peas (mung dal)
2½ cups water
2-inch piece fresh ginger, peeled and grated
½ teaspoon ground turmeric
2 tablespoons ghee, butter, or sunflower oil

4 garlic cloves, thinly sliced
2 teaspoons black mustard seeds
1 teaspoon cumin seeds
6 fresh red Thai or serrano chilies
Salt to taste
Chopped fresh cilantro for garnish

Rinse the split peas until the water runs clear. Place in a saucepan and cover with the water. Bring to a boil. Scoop off and discard the foam that rises to the top. Add the ginger and turmeric and simmer until the split peas become very soft and break up. The dal should be smooth and like a thick soup. The split peas will absorb a lot of water, so you may need to add more during the cooking time.

Melt the ghee, or butter, or heat the oil in a small skillet over medium heat. Add the garlic slices and fry until golden brown. Add the mustard seeds, cumin seeds, and chilies; when the mustard seeds start to "pop" (after just a few seconds), remove from heat and pour over the split peas. Stand back slightly, as the mixture will crackle and spit. Add salt and garnish with cilantro.

KASHMIRI GOBI

This is a northern Indian way of cooking cauliflower, using cashew nuts and cayenne pepper together with an aromatic tomato sauce. It makes a good main dish, along with Nalagarh Brinjal (page 66) and Orange Rice (page 67).

SERVES 4–6

1 large onion, chopped	½ teaspoon ground cloves
4 garlic cloves	1 teaspoon ground cardamom
2-inch piece fresh ginger, peeled	4 bay leaves
3 tomatoes, chopped	1 teaspoon sugar
6 tablespoons oil	1 teaspoon salt
1 large cauliflower, separated into florets	
1 teaspoon ground turmeric	*Garnish*
1 teaspoon cayenne pepper	¼ cup cashew nuts, toasted
1 teaspoon ground cinnamon	¼ cup raisins

Purée the onion, garlic, ginger, and tomatoes together in a food processor.

Heat the oil in a large, heavy saucepan over medium heat and sauté the cauliflower until it is beginning to brown and soften. Remove from the pan with a slotted spoon.

In the saucepan, sauté the onion mixture with the turmeric and cayenne for 3 minutes. Add the cinnamon, cloves, cardamom, bay leaves, sugar, and salt.

Return the cauliflower to the pan and turn to coat well and heat through.

Serve garnished with the toasted cashew nuts and raisins.

Kashimiri Gobi, Nalagarh Brinjal, and Narangi Pulao were among the many dishes we ate while photographing Nalagarh Fort, the ancestral home of the Maharaja Vijayendra Singh, situated in the foothills of the Himalayas. We went there just before it was opened as a hotel; the cooks were old family retainers, and must by now be cooking some of these recipes for the hotel guests. Kashmiri Gobi is a recipe brought into the family by the Maharani, who came from the western side of Kashmir, which is now part of Pakistan.

Kashmiri Gobi

NALAGARH BRINJAL

This sidedish of eggplant in yogurt is quite luxurious, as is appropriate for the table of a maharaja.

SERVES 4–6

1 large eggplant, cut into rounds
   ½ inch thick
1 teaspoon ground turmeric
Salt to taste
5 tablespoons sunflower oil
2 cups yogurt
½ cup heavy cream

3 garlic cloves, crushed
1-inch piece fresh ginger, peeled and
   crushed
2 green Thai or serrano chilies
Handful of fresh cilantro leaves,
   chopped, for garnish

Sprinkle the eggplant slices with the turmeric and some salt. Heat the oil to almost smoking in a skillet over medium heat and fry the eggplant slices, a few at a time, until well browned. Transfer to paper towels to drain.

In a food processor, blend the yogurt, cream, garlic, ginger, and chilies. Place the eggplant slices on a flat dish and pour over the mixture.

Serve garnished with cilantro.

Above left **Narangi Pulao and Fruit Lassi (page 83)**

Above right **A man smokes a hookah at dusk on Dal Lake**

NARANGI PULAO

Serves 4–6

Orange Rice

3 oranges, scrubbed
6 cups water
3 tablespoons canola oil
1 tablespoon sugar
2 onions, very thinly sliced
8 cloves
Seeds from 8 cardamom pods
Salt to taste
2 cups basmati rice, washed, soaked,
 and drained
1 pound potatoes, peeled and cut
 into small dice
4 tablespoons oil
1 onion, puréed

4 garlic cloves, puréed
3 cloves
Seeds from 3 cardamom pods
1 cinnamon stick, crushed
1 teaspoon cayenne pepper
4 bay leaves
1 cup whole-milk yogurt
Juice of 1 lemon

Garnish

1 tablespoon butter
12 cashew nuts
12 whole almonds
Rose water for sprinkling (optional)

Narangi pulao can be eaten as a side dish with almost any curry or dal. The traditional way to serve it at Nalagarh is with a layer of fried potato-and-yogurt mixture sandwiched between the rice, making it into a whole meal.

The dish is similar to the rice we ate in Oman (see page 40), cooked in an essentially Persian style; the similarity again reflects the historical family connections with lands farther to the west in the days before the partition of India.

To make the Orange Rice: Peel the oranges and cut the rind into thin strips. Chop the oranges into dice, discarding the seeds and pith. Put the rind with the water, 1 tablespoon of the oil, and the sugar into a pan and boil for 5 minutes.

Meanwhile, sauté the onion, cloves, and cardamom seeds in the remaining 2 tablespoons oil until brown. Season with salt, then add the drained rice. Stir to coat the rice, then add the orange rind and boiling water. Cook until the rice is tender, about 12 minutes.

Sauté the potatoes in half the oil in a skillet over medium heat until crispy and set aside. Sauté the puréed onion and garlic in the remaining oil until brown. Add the cloves, cardamom, cinnamon, cayenne, and bay leaves, and cook for 1 minute. Add the yogurt and lemon juice. Cook slowly over low heat for 10 minutes, then stir in the potatoes. Meanwhile, sauté the cashew nuts and almonds in the butter.

To complete the dish, place half the rice on a flat dish, pour on the yogurt and potato mixture, then put the other half of the rice on top. Serve garnished with the fried nuts and the orange pieces. Sprinkle with rose water.

To serve Orange Rice as a side dish, garnish with the cubes of orange and the fried nuts.

Potato *bondas* make a wonderful snack or starter and keep for several days, so it's worth preparing quite a lot at a time. We made a whole tinful to take skiing in Kashmir, filling our ski-jacket pockets with them at the beginning of each day so that we could snack on them during ski-lift rides. As the balls are quite fragile, they also provided an extra incentive not to fall over.

The *bondas* are supposed to be very spicy, so they are particularly good to eat on the cold snow slopes. When I offered one to a Scandinavian skier sharing my chair lift, he found it excessively hot and, as soon as we got off, grabbed mouthfuls of snow to relieve his burning mouth. This recipe has been considerably toned down to make a milder version — if you want to spice it up again, just add more chili.

Potato Bondas, with Green Coconut Chutney (page 84)

POTATO BONDAS

These potato fritters are particularly good served with Green Coconut Chutney (page 84).

SERVES 4–6

Batter
6 tablespoons chickpea flour (gram flour or besan)
Pinch of salt
Pinch of hing (asafetida)
1 teaspoon ground turmeric
1 teaspoon chili powder
Water as needed

Bondas
Oil for deep frying
2 pounds potatoes, peeled, cooked, and mashed
2 tablespoons sunflower oil
¼ teaspoon salt
2 teaspoons sugar
4 teaspoons shredded dried coconut
5–10 green Thai or serrano chilies, finely chopped
2 pinches of hing (asafetida)
2-inch piece fresh ginger, minced
1 teaspoon sesame seeds
1 teaspoon garam masala
Juice of 1 lime
Handful of minced fresh cilantro

Mix all the batter ingredients together in a bowl, adding water a spoonful at a time until a thick paste forms.

Mix all the rest of the ingredients together and mold by hand into balls about the size of a golf ball.

Heat the oil for deep frying. When the oil is hot enough to cause a drop of the batter to sizzle and bubble rapidly, dip each ball of mixture in the batter and deep fry the bondas in 2–3 batches, turning regularly, for 5–10 minutes, or until golden brown all over. Drain on paper towels and serve hot or cold.

For convenience, the balls may instead be flattened out a bit and panfried, turning once.

EASTERN INDIA

Eastern India attracts far fewer foreign tourists than the west. When we went to the annual Sonepur Elephant Mela (fair) on a tributary of the Ganges near Patna in Bihar, we were among only a small handful of foreigners. The Mela, along with a full-moon pilgrimage, attracts just as many revelers, traders, and devotees as the Camel Mela does on the same night over in Rajasthan (see page 86), yet here nearly all of them are locals. There is plenty of interesting food available from the dozens of stalls. Also fascinating is the sight of so many elephants being manipulated between surging crowds of humanity. Occasionally, an elephant breaks free, causing scenes of panic and great amusement, but most of the time they are occupied in eating or being washed, decorated, or otherwise pampered, and maintain a regal air of disregard for all around them.

From Patna we traveled by train to Calcutta, sitting next to a man whose family owned a small hotel there (his card described it as "located in posh area"). We decided to give it a go, and found the East West Guest House the perfect base from which to explore the extraordinary city. It was located not only in a pleasantly "posh" area but also above a first-rate street café.

On our way back to Delhi, we spent a few days in Varanasi, that most holy of Hindu cities, on the holiest river, the Ganges. We arrived at night and strolled along the riverbank beneath the towering walls of the old city, past a series of steps, or ghats, leading to the water. Turning a corner, we were confronted with a scene of medieval intensity. The walls were illuminated by golden light from roaring fires; crowds of wailing, hooded people blocked the way; men in loincloths scurried here and there; priests were chanting and ringing bells; and incense wafted about, together with a smell of burning flesh. The fires were funeral pyres: We had reached the burning-ghat of Manikamika.

We fell in love with Varanasi, and have returned several times — once during Divali, the Hindu Festival of Lights. The narrow alleyways and courtyards were lit by thousands of candles and butter lamps, and echoed to the sounds of temple singing and "bottle bomb" fireworks. In the midst of the carnival-style festivities, we watched four old men, seemingly oblivious to all the activity, carry a large dead cow down to the Ganges. They precariously floated it out into the river between two small boats, and silently let it sink into the current. They returned to the shore without exchanging a word, then slipped off separately into the shadows.

A ferry across the Ganges at Varanasi

CALCUTTA EGGPLANT

SERVES 4–6

1 large onion, chopped

12 garlic cloves

6 green Thai or serrano chilies

6 tablespoons sunflower oil

3 teaspoons ground paprika

½ teaspoon cayenne pepper

1 teaspoon ground turmeric

1 pound Japanese eggplants, cut into quarters lengthwise

3 teaspoons tamarind paste

Water as needed

2 teaspoons finely chopped jaggery or packed brown sugar

Handful of cilantro leaves, chopped

Purée the onion, garlic, and chilies in a food processor.

Heat the oil in a large, heavy saucepan over medium heat and fry the onion mixture with the paprika, cayenne, and turmeric for 3 minutes.

Add the eggplant and cook for 5 minutes. Dissolve the tamarind paste in a little water and stir in, then add the jaggery or brown sugar. Cook until the eggplant becomes soft.

Serve garnished with lots of fresh cilantro, and accompanied with chapatis.

This is one of the dishes we ate regularly in Calcutta, sitting on low wooden benches under one of the huge shade-giving board trees on the pavement beneath our guest house. The street café, operating out of a typically Calcuttan hole in the wall, had the added bonus of being so popular with taxi drivers that we could always be sure of a cab right after our meal. The food was so good that we rarely ate anywhere else.

Above **The Calcuttan "hole-in-the-wall" café**

Right **Calcutta Eggplant**

ORISSAN JAGDISH SAAG ALOO

Serves 4–6

6 tablespoons vegetable oil

2 tablespoons red pepper flakes

2 teaspoons black mustard seeds

5 potatoes, peeled, cubed, and
soaked in cold water for a few
hours, then drained well

2 tablespoons fresh fenugreek leaves

6 garlic cloves, crushed

1-inch piece fresh ginger, peeled and
minced

3 green Thai or serrano chilies,
minced

1 pound fresh spinach, stemmed and
finely chopped

Water as needed

Heat the oil in a large, heavy saucepan over medium heat and stir in the pepper flakes. Add the mustard seeds and cook them briefly until they pop. Add the potatoes a spoonful at a time, so as not to lower the heat of the oil too much, and stir-fry for 5 minutes. Add the fenugreek leaves, garlic, ginger, and chilies. Continue to stir-fry until the potatoes start to break up. Add the spinach and a little water. Serve when the spinach has wilted.

We rented a house for a few weeks on the coast of Orissa, in the eccentric village of Gopalpur-on-Sea. During our stay there, we passed several jovial evenings in the homes of local minor dignitaries, but most of our meals were enjoyed in the hub of Gopalpur's nightlife, the Jagdish Coffee Hotel.

This was not a hotel at all, but a one-room café open to the street. The kitchen received a constant supply of firewood, water, vegetables, and milk,

and delivered an equally constant supply of great food. We grew especially fond of the two dishes on these pages, the spinach and potato dish, Saag Aloo, and Vegetable Masala.

The Bay of Bengal at Gopalpur-on-Sea

MIXED-VEGETABLE MASALA

This is a basic mixed-vegetable masala, using fried whole spices, chopped vegetables, and tomatoes. The vegetables used can vary according to taste and availability.

SERVES 4–6

6 tablespoons sunflower oil

2 teaspoons black mustard seeds

2 teaspoons cumin seeds

2 teaspoons coriander seeds

6 green Thai or serrano chilies, minced

12 garlic cloves, crushed

1 onion, thinly sliced

2-inch piece fresh ginger, peeled and minced

1 teaspoon ground turmeric

2 carrots, peeled, cut into quarters lengthwise, then chopped

2 zucchini, cut into quarters lengthwise, then chopped

4 ounces long beans or green beans, chopped

1 cabbage (1 pound), cored and chopped

1½ cups green peas (fresh or frozen)

8 ounces tomatoes, chopped

Handful of fresh cilantro sprigs, stemmed (reserve stems)

2 tablespoons tomato paste

Water as needed

Heat the oil to almost smoking in a large, heavy saucepan over medium heat, then sauté – in this order – the mustard seeds, cumin, coriander, chilies, garlic, onion, ginger, and turmeric, adding each in rapid succession so the seeds have enough time to pop without burning.

When the onion begins to soften, add all the remaining vegetables except the tomatoes, together with the cilantro stems, and sauté for a few minutes until the cabbage begins to brown and the other vegetables soften.

Add the tomatoes and cook for 1 minute. Add the tomato paste and reduce the heat, adding a little water to allow the vegetables to simmer until cooked.

Serve with rice and garnish with cilantro leaves.

SOUTHERN INDIA

Southern India includes the Deccan plateau; the plains of the Malabar and Coromandel coasts and the mountainous Eastern and Western Ghats that separate them; and, in the far south, the flat lands of Tamil Nadu. While the food of the coasts inevitably involves a lot of seafood, vegetarian options are still plentiful; in Tamil Nadu, as in Gujarat, vegetarianism is the norm. Much use is made of coconut in creamy sauces and nutty chutneys; rice grows everywhere and is served in copious amounts at every meal. The Deccan does not have the wealth that the coastal states have accumulated through generations of sea trading, so the food there is often more basic. The exception is Bangalore, the capital of Karnataka, which has blossomed into a dynamic and prosperous city thanks to its booming information technology industry. Its new wealth has attracted India's first Kentucky Fried Chicken outlet and many fast-food imitators, but thankfully there has been demand for fine new Indian restaurants, too.

We left Bangalore by the night train for the north of Karnataka, where, after a first-rate meal and a good night's sleep, we woke up to find an India from another century. We drove past acres of sunflowers to the sleepy town of Badami, whose tree-lined avenues were almost devoid of motorized traffic; bullock carts, horse-drawn tongas, and bicycles were the only company for our car. In the cliffs above the town are some fifth-century caves full of exquisite stone carvings depicting scenes from Hindu and Buddhist mythology. As the Moguls fought their way south in the sixteenth century, destroying such images, they missed these, which are almost intact today. Despite such treasures, relatively few foreigners pass through Badami, and tourists are still a novelty. From Badami, we drove south to the ruins of Vijayanagar at Hampi; these have not survived years of conflict as well as Badami has, but their sheer size and their setting among desolate, boulder-strewn hills make them just as impressive.

In Kerala, vegetables come immersed in fragrant coconut cream laced with spices, while in Tamil Nadu we ate well on numerous filling dishes served on a fresh banana leaf. As soon as any one of the many ingredients on the leaf is eaten, a man appears and replaces it with more of the same; only when one folds over the leaf is there an escape from the unending meal. However, more than the plethora of vegetable and dal dishes, it is the chutneys and raitas that we remember most, and we have put the tastiest of them in this chapter.

An elephant in the morning mists in Tamil Nadu's Mudumalai Sanctuary

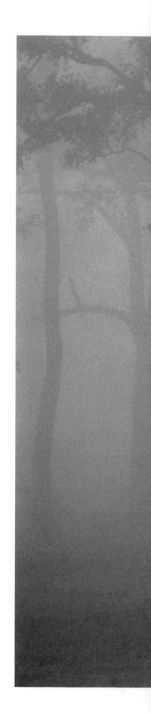

POTATO AND PEANUT PAWA

Pawa is a type of flat rice, available in Indian markets.

SERVES 4–6

4 tablespoons vegetable oil

1 teaspoon black mustard seeds

⅓ cup raw peanuts

3 potatoes, peeled, diced, and boiled
   until soft

1 teaspoon sesame seeds

½ teaspoon ground turmeric

½ teaspoon chili powder

1 green Thai or serrano chili,
   minced

1 tablespoon shredded, dried
   coconut

Salt and sugar to taste

½ cup pawa (dried flat rice), rinsed
   and drained

Large handful of fresh cilantro leaves

Heat the oil in a large skillet over medium heat. Add the mustard seeds and cook until they pop, then add the peanuts. When they begin to brown, add the drained potatoes, sesame seeds, and turmeric. Fry until the potatoes begin to brown. Add the chili powder, green chili, coconut, salt, and sugar; mix gently.

Remove from heat and mix in the pawa flakes. Return to the heat and fry until the pawa flakes are heated through.

Add the cilantro leaves and either eat warm or keep in a sealed container for your train journey.

CACHUMBERS

A cachumber is a raw vegetable accompaniment that usually includes onion; we give the classic version with tomato.

SERVES 4–6

1 medium-to-large red onion, finely
   diced

3 tomatoes, cut into small cubes

Juice of 1 lime

1 tablespoon fresh cilantro leaves,
   chopped

Salt to taste

Mix all the ingredients in a bowl.

In the town of Badami, we found people friendly and hospitable — so much so that when we enthused about a lunch we ate in a café, we were not allowed to pay for it. The day we left Badami, we persuaded the café owners to let us pay for a container of food to take away with us. The dish was very simple, using an ingredient we had seen often in markets but had never known how to use. This was *pawa*: dried, flattened flakes of rice.

Quite unappetizing in its raw state, once brought to life with oil, spices, potatoes, and peanuts, pawa becomes a great snack food. It is very popular in southern India — families cook it up and take it with them in stainless steel tins to snack on during long train journeys.

The entrance to the
cave temples at Badami
in Karnataka

COCONUT CABBAGE

SERVES 4–6

4 tablespoons sunflower oil

2-inch piece fresh ginger, peeled and
    cut into matchsticks

2 green Thai or serrano chilies,
    thinly sliced

8 curry leaves

2 teaspoons black mustard seeds

½ teaspoon ground turmeric

1 cabbage (about 1½ pounds), cored
    and finely shredded

2 tablespoons shredded, dried
    coconut

1 teaspoon sugar

1 teaspoon salt

Make sure you have all the ingredients ready. Heat the sunflower oil in a wok
over high heat and add the ginger, chilies, and curry leaves. Fry for 1 minute.

Add the mustard seeds and turmeric, and when the mustard seeds start to
pop, add the cabbage. Stirring constantly, fry until the cabbage starts to wilt.

Add the coconut, stirring well until it begins to toast. Add the sugar and salt.
Serve immediately.

79

The chickpea dish given
here may be called either
chana batura or *chana
masala*. As *chana batura*,
it is served with deep-
fried *batura* bread and
makes a popular fast-
food dish in Bombay
cafés. As *chana masala*,
it can be a side dish,
along with vegetables
and rice or chapatis, and
appears all over India.

CHANA IN A THICK, SPICY GRAVY

SERVES 4–6

Handful of fresh cilantro leaves,
  chopped
Handful of fresh mint leaves,
  chopped
3 onions, chopped
12 garlic cloves
2-inch piece fresh ginger
1 teaspoon cumin seeds
1 teaspoon coriander seeds
2-inch piece cinnamon stick
7 small, dried red peppers
10 black peppercorns
2 bay leaves

1 teaspoon ground turmeric
4 tablespoons ghee, butter, or
  sunflower oil
2 tablespoons tomato paste
1¼ cups dried chickpeas, soaked
  overnight and boiled until soft
2 potatoes, peeled, cooked, and
  chopped small
1 small bunch spinach, stemmed and
  chopped
Water as needed
Salt to taste

In a food processor, process the cilantro, mint, onions, garlic, and ginger to
a paste.

Toast the cumin and coriander seeds, cinnamon, red peppers, peppercorns,
bay leaves, and turmeric in a small skillet over medium heat, tossing constantly
to avoid burning, then grind them all in a spice grinder into a dry masala.

Melt the ghee in a large, heavy saucepan over medium heat and fry the paste
for 3 minutes. Add the dry masala and fry for another minute. Add the tomato
paste and cook for 3 minutes more.

Add the drained chickpeas and chopped potatoes, followed by the spinach,
and cook until the latter is wilted. Add water as needed to form a thick gravy.
Season with salt and serve.

A woman worships at
the giant effigy of
Ganesh, the elephant-
headed Hindu god, at
Hampi in northern
Karnataka

COCHIN COCONUT MASALA

Serves 4–6

5 small, dried red peppers

2 tablespoons white poppy seeds

2 tablespoons coriander seeds

1 teaspoon cumin seeds

5 cloves

10 black peppercorns

½ cup shredded, dried coconut, toasted in a hot pan until just brown

Water as needed

6 tablespoons sunflower oil

1 teaspoon black mustard seeds

1 teaspoon cumin seeds

Pinch of hing (asafetida)

5–10 fresh green Thai or serrano chilies, cut into thin strips

1 teaspoon ground turmeric

12 curry leaves

1 large onion, thinly sliced

1 large sweet potato, peeled and cut into chunks

2 zucchini, cut into chunks

8 ounces daikon (about 1 cup), peeled and cut into chunks

4 ounces okra, cut in half lengthwise

4 ounces green beans, cut in half

1¼ cups (14 ounces) coconut milk

Juice of 1 lime

Salt to taste

Toast the red peppers, poppy seeds, coriander seeds, cumin seeds, cloves, and peppercorns in a small skillet over medium heat, tossing constantly to avoid burning. Let them cool, then grind in a spice grinder. Mix with the toasted coconut and a little water to make a paste.

Heat the oil in a large, heavy saucepan over medium heat and sauté the mustard seeds, cumin seeds, hing, chilies, turmeric, and curry leaves, then add the onion. Sauté until the onion is tender. Add the sweet potato and sauté for 3 minutes.

Add the spice paste and all the other vegetables, stirring everything for 5 minutes. Then add the coconut milk, reduce the heat, and cook until the vegetables are tender, adding a little more water if necessary.

Finally, add the lime juice and a little salt.

After a minor accident in Cochin in Kerala, I spent a night in the hospital. The next day, my bed was needed for another patient so I had to transfer to a hotel, but I was told not to walk for three days. I was carried around on a stretcher through the streets until a suitable hotel was found.

I hadn't considered the complication of getting food without being able to walk — but I needn't have worried. Each day, medical students arrived to change my dressing and supply me with fresh food from their canteen, assuring me that it was merely their duty to attend the wounded.

While I was laid up in bed, this dish was something I looked forward to every day. I loved the way the vegetables were cut, as well as the tastes — it felt as if someone was really looking after me.

Enormous Chinese-style fishing nets, used in Cochin, are seen here silhouetted against the evening sky

FRUIT LASSI

This refreshing and cooling yogurt drink makes a perfect accompaniment to a spicy curry, and can be sweet or savory. In the café, we use mango, but you can use any soft fruit, such as banana.

SERVES 4–6

2 cups (16 ounces) whole-milk
   yogurt
1 cup ice water
1 cup cold milk
½ teaspoon ground cardamom seeds

1 tablespoon rose water
2 mangoes, peeled, cut from pit,
   and cubed, or 5 ripe bananas,
   peeled and sliced
Toasted, sliced almonds, for serving

Put all the ingredients, except the almonds in a blender or food processor and blend until smooth. Serve with ice cubes and sprinkled with the almonds.

GREEN COCONUT CHUTNEY

Serves 4–6

Handful of fresh cilantro leaves	2 cups shredded, dried coconut
Handful of fresh mint leaves	Juice of 2 limes
1 garlic clove	Water as needed
1-inch piece fresh ginger, peeled and coarsely chopped	1 teaspoon sugar
2 green Thai or serrano chilies	1 teaspoon salt

In a food processor, blend the cilantro, mint, garlic, ginger, chilies, coconut, and lime juice until they form a paste. Add just enough water to make a moist (but not wet) chutney. Mix in the sugar and salt.

If you make this in advance, the coconut will absorb the water, so simply add more water to get the desired consistency before serving.

SWEET DATE AND TAMARIND CHUTNEY

Serves 4–6

1½ cups dates, pitted and chopped	1 teaspoon honey
2 teaspoons tamarind paste	1 cup water
2 teaspoons cumin seeds, toasted in a small skillet	Salt to taste

Put all the ingredients in a food processor and process until well combined.

In India, no meal is complete without a chutney. There are hundreds of different recipes, for both fresh and cooked versions. Chutneys based on coconut are more common in the south, fruit chutneys in the north and west.

Raita is the term used for a variety of cooling yogurt-based accompaniments. We've chosen two examples, one savory, one sweet.

CUCUMBER AND MINT RAITA

SERVES 4–6

1 cup plain yogurt

Water as needed

½ cucumber, peeled and cut into
    small cubes

4 sprigs mint, stemmed and
    chopped

¼ teaspoon ground cumin

½ teaspoon sugar

Salt and pepper to taste

Paprika for garnsih

Whisk the yogurt with a little water to thin it to a spoonable consistency. Add all of the remaining ingredients except the paprika. Mix well.

Chill the raita, if you have the time. Sprinkle the paprika over the top before serving.

BANANA RAITA

SERVES 4–6

1 cup plain yogurt

1 teaspoon black mustard seeds

3 bananas, peeled and cut into
    ½-inch thick slices

½ teaspoon sugar

1 green Thai or serrano chili, thinly
    sliced

Salt to taste

Whisk the yogurt with a little water to thin it to a spoonable consistency. Toast the black mustard seeds in a small skillet over medium heat until they start to pop (cover the pan to prevent them jumping out). Add to the yogurt with all the remaining ingredients. Mix well.

WESTERN INDIA

The western states of Rajasthan and Gujarat are perhaps the most visually exciting in India. The stark beauty of desert landscapes is offset by brightly dressed and bejeweled women, and fine-featured men with noble moustaches and multi-colored turbans. Fairy-tale palaces and dramatic forts dominate towns of tiny blue, pink, and white houses squeezed together in narrow alleys. In the countryside, thatched mud huts have dung-floor courtyards populated with buffalo, camels, and goats.

Desert culture is experienced in all its glory at the annual Camel Mela (fair) and Hindu pilgrimage in the oasis village of Pushkar. The ingredients are seductive: tens of thousands of Rajasthanis in all their finery, almost as many camels in theirs, a holy lake surrounded by temples, long days of sunshine, and nights of moonlit skies and festivities. The first time I went, my companion and I left our passports behind for safety in our Delhi hotel — breaching a law that requires foreigners to carry their documents. On being discovered without passports, we were arrested. Thus began a two-week ordeal.

For several days, we were kept in an overcrowded cell, manacled hand and foot, and very worried. We were then taken in chains under police escort back to Delhi, an eighteen-hour train journey that we spent locked to the luggage rack. Even once our passports were found to be in order, we were told we had to return to the desert to be sentenced for the crime of not carrying them with us. Meanwhile, we had a day to spend in Delhi. None of our three police escorts had been to the capital before. A bargain was struck. We would give them a day out in the city and buy some presents for their wives, and they would put our chains in a bag. A good day was had by all.

Back in Pushkar we were given a clean cell all to ourselves — and were treated to fine feasts, delivered from the kitchens of our new friends' wives. At our trial, we pleaded guilty and were released unconditionally. The policemen now insisted we stay on as guests in their homes. We met their wives, proudly dressed in the saris and bangles from Delhi, and complimented them on their cooking. With a mix of Hindi, English, and much pointing and laughing, we gathered some of the recipes in this chapter.

Some of our trips produce pleasures less fraught with excitement. One of the most interesting parts of Rajasthan we visited was Shekhawati: a sand-blown region, home in the fourteenth century to prosperous Muslim merchants who built great mansions, or *havelis,* lavishly decorated with carvings and murals. Later generations abandoned these desert homes for the more sophisticated pleasures of the cities. Today, the *havelis* are occupied by caretakers or local families, and most, sadly, are in a state of neglect.

The Pushkar Camel Mela (fair)

The Rann of Kutch is a wild district of Gujarat bordering Pakistan. The desert tribes are semi-nomadic, travelling in family groups with camels and goats. The capital, Bhuj, feels like a town from another century, although it is only three hours by air from Bombay. On our way back to Bombay, we stopped in Junagadh to climb the 10,000 stone steps up the temple-strewn Girnar Hill. Our ascent coincided with the festival of Shivaratri and its tens of thousands of pilgrims — many of them naked, ash-covered *sadhus* (holy men) who were not at all keen on being photographed. It was hard even to see a patch of ground in the throng of humanity, and the climb seemed quite effortless as the great crowd swept us with it up the mountain.

SAAG PANEER

This spinach and cheese dish is our all-time favorite recipe, and we have eaten it in practically every state in India. There are many ways of cooking it, but in our opinion this is the best. The Indian cheese paneer *is pretty tasteless in its raw state, but fried and soaked in sauce it is fantastic.* Paneer *is widely available in Indian stores.*

SERVES 4–6

2 bunches fresh spinach, stemmed and shredded	6 garlic cloves, crushed
Water as needed	4 green Thai or serrano chilies, minced
3–4 tablespoons ghee, butter, or sunflower oil	2 teaspoons garam masala
14 ounces paneer, cut into ½-inch dice	¼ teaspoon freshly grated nutmeg
2-inch piece ginger, peeled and crushed	1 cup heavy cream
	Large handful of fresh cilantro leaves, chopped
	Salt to taste

Cook the spinach with a small quantity of water, just enough to keep it from sticking, until wilted. Remove from heat.

Melt the ghee or butter, or heat the oil, in a heavy saucepan over medium heat and fry the paneer until it is golden brown, turning it occasionally to make sure all sides are cooked.

With a slotted spoon, remove the paneer from the pan. Add the ginger, garlic, and chilies to the saucepan (there should be enough ghee, butter, or oil left in the pan; if not, add a little more). Sauté for 1 minute, stirring constantly.

Add the cooked spinach and any of its liquid. Stir and simmer for 10 minutes.

Return the fried paneer to the pan, together with the garam masala and nutmeg. Simmer for 10 minutes.

Add the cream, cilantro, and salt. Gently simmer for 5 minutes.

Serve with a raita (page 85) and rice cooked with cinnamon, cardamom, and cloves (1-inch piece cinnamon stick, 3 cardamom pods, and 3 cloves for 2 cups of rice).

At the luxurious end of the comfort scale, we photographed royal palaces in Rajasthan and Gujarat that have been converted into Heritage Hotels. Some of these are former residences of undiluted opulence, others more modest ancestral homes.

In the superbly romantic courtyard of Shiv Niwas Palace in Udaipur, we ate one of the best *saag paneer* dishes we tasted in India — substantially better than the meal we had the following night in the more famous and absurdly picturesque Lake Palace Hotel.

Saag Paneer

ALOO GOBI OF RAJASTHAN

SERVES 4–6

4 tablespoons ghee, butter, or
    sunflower oil
Pinch of hing (asafetida)
Pinch of fenugreek seeds
1 teaspoon fennel seeds
Handful of fresh fenugreek leaves,
    minced
Handful of fresh cilantro stems,
    minced

6 green Thai or serrano chilies,
    finely chopped
1 teaspoon ground turmeric
1 head cauliflower, separated into
    florets and blanched
3 potatoes, peeled, cubed, and
    blanched
Salt and pepper to taste
Water as needed

Melt the ghee or butter or heat the oil in a heavy saucepan over medium heat
and sauté the hing, fenugreek seeds, and fennel seeds for 1 minute. Add the
fenugreek and cilantro and cover the pan for a few seconds.

    Add the chilies and turmeric with the cauliflower and potatoes, and stir to
coat. Add salt, pepper, and a little water to loosen the mixture. Reduce heat to
low and cover until all is cooked.

Aloo gobi (cauliflower
and potato) is one of the
ubiquitous dishes of
India; it comes in
hundreds — probably
thousands — of forms. In
fact, as the name
suggests, cauliflower and
potato are the only
essential ingredients;
beyond these, the
possibilities are endless.

Above **Brightly dressed
women in a Rajasthani
marketplace**

Right **The blue houses
of Jodhpur seen
through a narrow
window in the Red Fort**

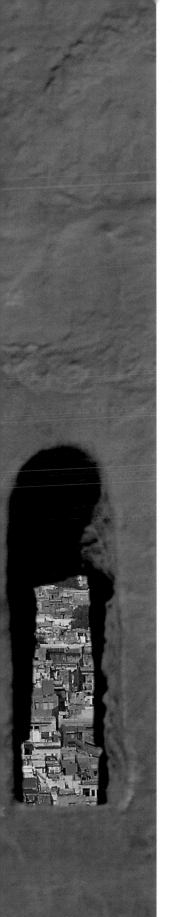

ROOT VEGETABLES IN A SPICY MINT SAUCE

We enjoyed this dish in Udaipur, on the banks of the lake overlooking the Lake Palace. You can use any root vegetable, but plenty of fresh mint is essential. Serve with rice and the Savory Fruit Salad on page 95.

SERVES 4–6

4 teaspoons coriander seeds	4 potatoes, peeled and cubed
1 teaspoon ground turmeric	6 tomatoes, puréed in a food
2 teaspoons cayenne pepper	processor
2-inch piece fresh ginger, peeled and coarsely chopped	2 large handfuls of fresh mint leaves, chopped
Water as needed	Small handful of fresh cilantro leaves, chopped
5 tablespoons sunflower oil	Salt to taste
6 turnips, cubed	

Toast the coriander seeds in a small skillet until they start to brown, then grind to a powder.

Place the ground coriander, turmeric, cayenne, and ginger in a food processor and blend with a little water until a paste forms.

Heat the oil in a heavy saucepan over medium heat and fry the turnips and potatoes until they start to soften. Add the spice paste and stir until the vegetables are coated. Add the tomatoes and a little water to make a sauce. Simmer until the vegetables are tender.

Add the mint, cilantro, and salt. Stir to combine and serve immediately.

DEEP-RED RAJASTHANI VEGETABLES IN A POPPY-SEED SAUCE

In this unusual dish, red cabbage, pumpkin, beets, and a spice mixture based on chilies and paprika combine to make a dish of vivid color, like the colors of Rajasthan itself. Poppy seeds are used to thicken the sauce.

SERVES 4–6

1 teaspoon fenugreek seeds	4 to 5 red Thai or serrano chilies,
2 tablespoons white poppy seeds	thinly sliced
1 tablespoon sweet paprika	2 cups cubed pie pumpkin
1 teaspoon ground coriander	5 beets, peeled and cubed
1 teaspoon amchoor (mango	⅓ small red cabbage, cored and
powder)	thinly shredded
1 teaspoon ground turmeric	6 tomatoes, pureed in a food
1 teaspoon ground cinnamon	processor
½ teaspoon ground cloves	Water as needed
2-inch piece fresh ginger, peeled and	1-inch square jaggery or 2 teaspoons
finely chopped	packed brown sugar
5 tablespoons sunflower oil	Salt to taste
1 red onion, thinly sliced	Chopped, fresh cilantro leaves, for
4 garlic cloves, crushed	garnish

In a small skillet toast the fenugreek seeds until they start to brown. Remove from the heat and add to the poppy seeds. Grind these in a spice grinder or using a mortar and pestle. Combine with all the remaining spices and the ginger.

Heat the oil in a large saucepan over medium heat and add the red onion, garlic, and chilies. Sauté for a few minutes. Add the pumpkin, beets, and red cabbage, and sauté until they start to soften. Add the spice mix and stir until the vegetables are coated. Add the pureed tomatoes and a little water until the sauce just covers the vegetables. Bring to a boil and simmer until the vegetables are tender and the sauce is reduced. Add the jaggery or brown sugar and salt. Stir to dissolve the sugar.

Garnish with chopped cilantro and serve with rice and Banana Raita (page 85).

Deep-Red Rajasthani Vegetables in a Poppy-Seed Sauce

We love *khadi*, which is a kind of yogurt soup, but we always imagined it would be difficult to make since the tastes seem to be so complex and intriguing. In fact, it's very easy, the secret being the blending of yogurt with chickpea flour (gram flour, or *besan*). *Khadi* makes a good starter or addition to any rice and vegetable meal.

KHADI

SERVES 4–6

2 cups yogurt

1½ tablespoons chickpea flour (gram flour, or besan)

4 green Thai or serrano chilies, chopped

1-inch piece fresh ginger, minced

2 teaspoons salt

2 teaspoons sugar

6 cups water

2 tablespoons ghee, butter, or sunflower oil

½ teaspoon black mustard seeds

½ teaspoon fenugreek seeds

½ teaspoon cumin seeds

½ teaspoon ground turmeric

6 cloves

1 tablespoon curry leaves

Pinch of hing (asafetida)

Handful of cilantro leaves, chopped

In a large bowl, whisk together the yogurt, chickpea flour, green chilies, ginger, salt, sugar, and water. Pour into a heavy pan, bring to a boil, reduce heat to low, and simmer for 20 minutes.

In a small skillet, melt the ghee or butter or heat the oil and sauté all the seeds until they pop. Add the turmeric, cloves, curry leaves, and hing and sauté for 30 seconds. Add this to the yogurt mixture, together with the cilantro. Stir and serve.

A zingy fruit salad makes a perfect accompaniment to a spicy curry.

SAVORY FRUIT SALAD

SERVES 4–6

2 apples, peeled, cored, and diced

2 carrots, peeled and diced

2 oranges, peeled and cut into small dice

½ cucumber, diced

1 papaya, peeled, seeded, and cut into small dice

Juice of 1 lemon

Handful of cilantro leaves, chopped

1 teaspoon cumin seeds, toasted and ground

½ teaspoon amchoor (mango powder)

½ teaspoon freshly ground black pepper

Salt to taste

A camel trader in Pushkar

Combine all the ingredients; refrigerate for about 30 minutes before serving.

GUJARATI CARROT SALAD

Hand-thrown village pots in western India

SERVES 4–6

2 teaspoons black mustard seeds
4 carrots, peeled and grated
1 teaspoon salt
Juice of 2 limes

Handful of fresh mint leaves,
    coarsely chopped

Toast the mustard seeds in a hot, small skillet until they start to pop (cover the pan with a lid or plate to prevent them jumping out). Remove from the heat and let cool. Combine with all the remaining ingredients.

GUJARATI PUMPKIN WITH TAMARIND

This Gujarati dish blends the sweetness of pumpkin and jaggery with the sourness of tamarind and amchoor. *It works well served with Coconut Cabbage (page 79) and Sweet Date and Tamarind Chutney (page 84).*

SERVES 4–6 WITH ACCOMPANIMENTS

- 4 garlic cloves
- 3 red Thai or serrano chilies
- 1 red onion, chopped
- 1 heaped teaspoon coriander seeds
- 2 teaspoons tamarind paste
- 2 teaspoons jaggery or packed brown sugar
- 3 tablespoons boiling water
- 3 tablespoons ghee, butter, or sunflower oil
- 1 large onion, thinly sliced

- One 2-pound pie pumpkin, peeled, seeded, and cubed
- ½ teaspoon ground turmeric
- ½ teaspoon ground black pepper
- 1 cup water
- 1 level teaspoon amchoor (mango powder)
- Salt to taste
- Large handful of fresh cilantro leaves, chopped

Put the garlic, chilies, and red onion in a blender or food processor and blend to a paste.

In a small skillet, toast the coriander seeds until they start to turn golden brown, then grind to a powder.

Dissolve the tamarind paste and jaggery or brown sugar in the boiling water.

In a large saucepan, melt the ghee or butter or heat the oil over medium heat. Add the onion and sauté until it starts to soften. Add the pumpkin and sauté until it starts to brown, stirring occasionally.

Add the chili paste, coriander, turmeric, and black pepper. Stir well and sauté for a few seconds. Add the tamarind water and the 1 cup water. Simmer gently, with the lid on, until the pumpkin is soft and most of the water has evaporated (but if it gets too dry at any time, add a little more water).

Add the amchoor, salt, and cilantro. Stir and simmer for 3 more minutes. Serve.

DIU CORN CURRY

Coconut milk is a perfect accompaniment to corn. This curry is delicious served with Gujarati Carrot Salad (page 96) and fresh mango chutney, or, for a larger meal, with Gujarati Pumpkin with Tamarind (page 97) as well.

SERVES 4–6

- 6 fresh ears corn, cut into 1-inch slices
- 2 large handfuls of fresh cilantro leaves, chopped, plus more for garnish
- 4 green Thai or serrano chilies
- 2-inch piece fresh ginger, peeled and chopped
- 2 garlic cloves
- 2 heaping tablespoons shredded, dried coconut
- Water as needed
- ⅞ cups coconut milk
- 2 tablespoons ghee, butter, or sunflower oil
- 2 teaspoons black mustard seeds
- 10 curry leaves
- Salt to taste

Cook the corn in salted boiling water until it starts to soften. Drain and return to the pan.

In a food processor, blend the cilantro, chilies, ginger, garlic, and coconut to a paste. Add the paste to the corn with enough water to make a sauce. Bring to a boil, reduce the heat, cover, and simmer for 10 minutes. Add the coconut milk and gently simmer for 5 minutes more.

Meanwhile, melt the ghee or butter or heat the oil in a small skillet over medium heat and add the mustard seeds. When they start to pop (a matter of seconds), add the curry leaves. Remove from heat and pour over the curry – it will make quite a loud crackling noise, so stand back a little. Add salt and garnish with more cilantro leaves.

Diu, a small island in the Arabian Sea, is just offshore from India's last "dry" state, Gujarat, but has a decidedly European taste for the pleasures of beer, wine, and spirits bequeathed to it by its long Portuguese history. Diu's pastel houses, narrow cobbled lanes, tavernas, and beaches are more reminiscent of the Mediterranean than India.

We discovered this dish while trying to drag ourselves away from the island after a welcome rest. A long-delayed train resulted in the station-master's inviting us to lunch in his home, and we ate with the family in a cobalt-blue courtyard just behind the station. We were quite disappointed when our train eventually arrived.

Diu Corn Curry, with Gujarati Carrot Salad (page 96)

NEPAL

The tourist "ghetto" of Thamil in Kathmandu offers a cosmopolitan choice of cuisine. Cafés, bistros, and restaurants line the streets to compete for the custom of hungry trekkers. On the most popular routes, tiny Himalayan villages provide banana pancakes, "Swiss" rösti, and pumpkin pie. In the remoter valleys, the choice is reduced to the Nepalese mainstay of *dal bhaat subji* or basic dal, rice, and vegetables. In the fertile lower valleys, these meals can be magnificent — creamy dals, healthy vegetables, good clean rice, and a range of chutneys and pickles. With increasing altitude and harshness of conditions, the choice of vegetables diminishes, and the rice is coarser. Altitude finally prevents rice cultivation altogether, and vegetarian meals consist of little more than potatoes with chilies and *tsampa* porridge. Even in such places, where life appears to be a constant battle against the elements, trekking in Nepal is made a pleasure by the warmth and good humor of the people as much as by the stunning landscapes.

Marigolds bloom under the Annapurna peaks

ANNAPURNA DAL BHAAT

This recipe is simple and a good way of making a lot of food relatively quickly.

SERVES 4–6

We ate *dal bhaat* in one form or another every day during a six-week circumnavigation of the Annapurna Mountains, and never got bored with it.

As rice was usually the cheapest ingredient in these meals, there was always plenty of it. To stretch the vegetable and dal dishes, they were made very spicy so that only a little was needed with each mouthful of rice.

In village homes, the meal is always eaten by mixing a little dal and vegetable or pickle with some rice and scooping it up with the right hand.

Dal
4 tablespoons ghee, butter, or
    sunflower oil
2 onions, thinly sliced
2-inch piece fresh ginger, minced
9 garlic cloves, crushed
2 teaspoons red pepper flakes
1 teaspoon ground turmeric
1½ cups dried red lentils
Water as needed
Salt to taste

Vegetables (Subji)
6 tablespoons sunflower oil

9 green Thai or serrano chilies, cut
    into thin strips
2-inch piece fresh ginger, minced
1 teaspoon ground cumin
1 teaspoon ground coriander seeds
½ teaspoon chili powder
1 teaspoon ground turmeric
6 small new potatoes, cut into
    ½-inch slices
3 carrots, peeled, cut into quarters
    lengthwise, and chopped
1 small cauliflower, cut into small
    florets
1½ cups shelled peas

To make the dal: Melt the ghee or butter or heat the oil in a large, heavy saucepan over medium heat and sauté the onions, ginger, and garlic until soft. Add the pepper flakes and turmeric, and sauté for 1 minute. Add the lentils and stir to coat them in the spices, then add enough water to cover them. Bring to a boil, reduce the heat, and simmer until the lentils are cooked, about 30 minutes, adding more water if necessary at any time to keep the dal the consistency of a thickish soup. Season with salt.

Towards the end of the lentil cooking time, cook the vegetables: Heat the oil in a large, heavy skillet over medium heat and sauté the chilies, ginger, and spices for 1 minute, stirring constantly. Add all the vegetables except the peas and cook until they begin to soften. Then add the peas with a little water, reduce the heat, and cook until tender.

Serve with plenty of steamed rice, any favorite pickles, and a salad of sliced daikon, fresh cilantro leaves, and chopped red onion.

SRI LANKA

Sri Lanka is a remarkably beautiful and deeply troubled island. Yet, considering the scale of the violence that is a daily reality for so many Sri Lankans, it is incredibly easy to be temporarily unaware of any trouble. We spent two weeks driving around the island's enchanting landscapes, meeting gentle, polite people, visiting serene Buddhist temple sites hosted by saffron-robed monks, and lazing on palm-fringed beaches. Nonetheless, there were sinister reminders of the island's tragedy lurking in the background, and our time was punctuated with police roadblocks, restricted travel, and an atmosphere of tension.

Self-drive car rental is difficult in Sri Lanka, so we shared our trip with a driver. There is a certain relief in being freed from the stress of driving in a foreign country, but it can be a complicated equation having to share almost every hour of every day with a man you have never met before. Our driver, Cyril, took his job very seriously: He was a faultless chauffeur, always smartly turned out and punctual. In fact, he took everything very seriously, and seemed to be bored beyond words by yet another drive around the island with a couple of excitable tourists — that is, until we declared our intention of climbing to the summit of Adam's Peak. The ascent of Adam's Peak is a demanding pilgrimage of which, as a devout Buddhist, Cyril thoroughly approved. At the 7,340-foot summit of the pyramid-shaped mountain there is a large "footprint" in the rock, left by the Buddha, or Adam, or St. Thomas, or Shiva, or geology, depending on your preference.

We certainly earned Cyril's friendship. The climb lasted all night. When we set off in the relative cool of the evening, the almost party atmosphere among the ascending pilgrims and the lure of thousands of steps winding up the mountain lined by tiny lights made a seductive combination. Several hours later in the chill of the pre-dawn air, the romance was fading fast. Our energy was replenished by the spectacular sunrise — not to mention the excitement of seeing, just outside the summit temple, a bright red British Mail—style mail box, with a daily collection at noon (which must demand an extremely fit postman). But then, disorientated as we were from lack of sleep, the descent, under an unrelenting tropical sun, down near-vertical steps, was punishing. We were as happy to see Cyril and his car waiting for us at the bottom as he had been to discover that his passengers were some sort of pilgrims.

A stilt fisherman at dusk in southern Sri Lanka

GREEN-VEGETABLE MALLUNG

Mallung, *which means "mixed up," is also the name of curries made with curry leaves, coconut, and chili.* Mallung *is most commonly made with green vegetables, of which there are many in Sri Lanka. Broccoli, for example, is abundant. This recipe can be made with any green vegetables, so feel free to substitute.*

Traditionally, mallung *should contain fish paste, made from pounded dried fish. In the café we do not, of course, use any fish products, but if you do eat fish, you might like to include Worcestershire sauce, which contains anchovies. The flavor is quite similar to that of fish paste, but more subtle.*

SERVES 4–6

4 tablespoons sunflower oil	Water as needed
1 large red onion, thinly sliced	3 cups coarsely shredded spinach
4 green Thai or serrano chilies, thinly sliced	14 ounces coconut milk
12 curry leaves	1 tablespoon Worcestershire sauce (optional)
1 tablespoon black mustard seeds	½ teaspoon ground saffron
12 ounces broccoli, cut into florets	Salt to taste
12 ounces yellow summer squash, peeled and cubed	Juice of 1 lime
½ cup shredded dried coconut	Chopped fresh cilantro leaves, for garnish

Heat the oil in a large saucepan over medium heat and sauté the onion for a few minutes. Add the chilies, curry leaves, and mustard seeds. Sauté until the mustard seeds pop.

Add the broccoli, squash, and coconut, and stir until the vegetables are coated in the spices and the coconut is toasted. Add enough water to partially cover the vegetables and simmer until they are just starting to soften.

Stir in the spinach, coconut milk, Worcestershire sauce (if using), and saffron. Gently simmer until all the vegetables are soft. Add salt and lime juice.

Garnish with cilantro and serve with Onion Sambol (page 111) and rice.

After we had earned the approval of our driver, Cyril, by our ascent of Adam's Peak, he made it his mission to search out the best food he could find, and eagerly explained how things were cooked. Lunch that day was a *mallung*, or mixture, of green vegetables in a coconut-cream sauce with black mustard seeds, green chilies, yellow saffron, and fresh curry leaves.

We ate the *mallung* while enjoying a grand view down towards the coastal plains. It tasted so delicious that we wondered if the setting, together with the healthy appetite from all our exercise, might be deceiving our senses, but every time we have cooked this dish since, its excellence has been confirmed.

Green–Vegetable Mallung

BEET AND BRINJAL BLACK CURRY

This recipe works well with Toasted Coconut and Pineapple Chutney (page 108), and the combination of yellow and red looks wonderful.

SERVES 4–6

2 red onions, coarsely chopped

3 garlic cloves

3 to 4 small dried red peppers

1 lemongrass stalk (white part only), chopped

2 teaspoons cumin seeds

2 teaspoons coriander seeds

1 scant teaspoon fennel seeds

4 tablespoons sunflower oil

1 pound beets, peeled and cubed

5 Japanese eggplants (brinjal), cut into quarters

1 cup vegetable stock

1 cup coconut milk

Salt and pepper to taste

1 cup cashew nuts

In a food processor, process the onions, garlic, chilies, and lemongrass to a pulp. Toast the cumin, coriander, and fennel seeds in a small skillet until they are dark brown (but not burnt, or they will taste bitter). Grind to a powder using a spice grinder or pestle and mortar.

Heat the oil in a large, heavy saucepan over medium heat. Add the onion paste and cook briskly for a few minutes, then add the ground spices, stirring constantly. When the spices are combined with the onion paste, add the beets and eggplants. Increase heat to high and sauté for another minute or two, stirring constantly.

Pour in the stock and bring to a boil, then reduce the heat, cover, and simmer until the vegetables are nice and soft. Add the coconut milk and cook for 5 minutes. Meanwhile, toast the cashew nuts in a small skillet until golden.

Season the curry with salt and pepper. Garnish with the toasted cashew nuts and serve with Toasted Coconut and Pineapple Chutney, and Coconut Rice (page 108).

In Sri Lanka, the main dishes are usually white curries, which are mild and creamy with lots of coconut milk; red curries, which are scarlet with ground chilies and tomatoes; or, delicious and most unusual-looking, black curries, darkened by spices toasted whole and ground to a powder.

We found this splendid recipe for Beet and Brinjal Black Curry at the delightfully "olde worlde" New Oriental Hotel in Galle, on the west coast of Sri Lanka. Built in 1865 as an officers' barracks, the hotel is famous not only for its atmospheric Victorian interiors, but also for its food.

Hill country near
Adam's Peak

COCONUT RICE

Serves 4–6

2 cups basmati rice

2 tablespoons butter

1 red onion, thinly sliced

4 green cardamom pods, lightly
   crushed

1 cup coconut milk

Water as needed

Salt to taste

Rinse the rice until the water runs clear.

Melt the butter in a medium saucepan over medium heat and sauté the onion until softened. Add the cardamom and rice and stir until the rice is coated in the butter. Add the coconut milk and enough water to cover the rice by ½ inch. Add salt.

Cover with a tight-fitting lid and bring to a boil, then reduce the heat and simmer gently until all water is absorbed.

Adjust the seasoning if necessary, fluffing the rice with a fork as you do so. Let stand for 10 minutes, still covered, before serving.

TOASTED COCONUT AND PINEAPPLE CHUTNEY

Pineapple works particularly well with chili, producing a delicious combination of sweet and sour.

Serves 4–6

½ cup shredded dried coconut

½ pineapple, peeled, cored, and
   cubed

3 green Thai or serrano chilies,
   thinly sliced

Juice of 1 lime

Salt to taste

Toast the coconut in a small skillet, stirring constantly, until it just starts to brown. Turn it out of the pan and set aside.

Combine the pineapple, chilies, lime juice, and salt. Pour over the coconut, mix well, and serve immediately.

Kandy is the capital of the hill country, and in many ways, it is also the spiritual capital. The Temple of the Tooth houses Sri Lanka's most important Buddhist relic, the Sacred Tooth of the Buddha, which is believed to have been taken from the flames of his funeral pyre and smuggled into Ceylon in the fourth century, hidden in the hair of a princess.

During morning and evening ceremonies, it is possible to "view" the tooth. In fact, you only see one of the many layers of casket in which it is housed, and needless to say, it is very heavily guarded. We ate this delicious leek and potato curry after the "viewing."

KANDY LEEK AND POTATO CURRY

SERVES 4–6

2 teaspoons cumin seeds

2 teaspoons coriander seeds

1 teaspoon fennel seeds

4 tablespoons sunflower oil

1 red onion, thinly sliced

5 garlic cloves, crushed

2-inch piece fresh ginger, minced

4 white potatoes, peeled, cubed, and blanched

4 large leeks (white part only), cut into 1-inch slices

2-inch piece cinnamon stick

½ teaspoon ground turmeric

1 teaspoon chili powder

8 curry leaves

1 tablespoon rice vinegar

Water as needed

1 cup coconut milk

Salt to taste

Fresh cilantro leaves, for garnish

Toast the cumin, coriander, and fennel seeds in a small skillet until they start to brown, then grind them to a powder using a spice grinder or pestle and mortar.

Heat the oil in a large, heavy pan over medium heat and sauté the onion, garlic, and ginger until soft. Add the potatoes and leeks and sauté until the vegetables start to brown. Add the ground toasted spices, cinnamon, turmeric, chili powder, curry leaves, and vinegar, stirring constantly to prevent sticking and to make sure that all the vegetables are coated in the spices.

Add enough water barely to cover the vegetables and simmer gently until the vegetables soften. Add the coconut milk and simmer for 5 minutes.

Add salt and sprinkle with the chopped cilantro leaves. Serve with Coconut Sambol (page 111) and rice.

A young monk takes a photograph with my camera at the Buddhist cliff carvings at Polonnaruwa

COCONUT SAMBOL

Serves 4–6

¾ cup shredded dried coconut
6 shallots, or 1 red onion, sliced
8 curry leaves

6 red Thai or serrano chillies (fewer
   if you don't like it too spicy)
Juice of 2 limes
Salt to taste

Soak the coconut in water until it swells and becomes fleshy. Drain. Place in a food processor with all the remaining ingredients, then blend until well combined. If the mixture seems dry, simply add a little water.

You can store this sambol in an airtight container in the fridge for a few days. The coconut will continue to absorb any moisture, so remoisten with a little lime juice and water before serving.

ONION SAMBOL

Serves 4–6

3 tablespoons sunflower oil
3 onions, finely chopped
4 garlic cloves, crushed
2 green Thai or serrano chilies,
   thinly sliced
1-inch cube piece fresh ginger,
   peeled and minced
4 green cardamom pods, lightly
   crushed

1 teaspoon ground cinnamon
2 teaspoons garam masala
1 teaspoon salt
1 teaspoon packed brown sugar
1 tablespoon rice vinegar
2 tablespoons tamarind paste,
   dissolved in ½ cup water
1 tablespoon Worcestershire sauce
   (optional)

Heat the oil in a heavy saucepan over medium heat and sauté the onions, garlic, chilies, and ginger until soft. Add all the spices and stir them into the onions.

Add all the remaining ingredients and gently simmer until reduced to a chutneylike consistency. In a food processor, process the mixture to a coarse purée. This sambol can be stored in an airtight container in the fridge for up to 1 month.

Sambols are spicy dry chutneys. They are served as accompaniments to most meals, or as a light meal, with roti bread or hoppers (rice-flour pancakes).

Southeast Asia

& China

All the countries of this region have a strong tradition of creative cooking using vegetables, nuts, spices, and soybean products. The results are quite different from the dishes that dominate Indian cooking. Pulses are used much less, and soybeans appear in the guise of tofu, tempeh, and of course soy sauce. Lemongrass, *galangal*, and lime leaves are the dominant spices. When traveling through most of this region, vegetarians can enjoy a great variety of dishes to accompany the ubiquitous staple of steamed white rice.

In some parts of the region travel is very easy. Our journeys around Bali and Lombok were made in the comfort of a private jeep, and we were never far from a luxury hotel. By contrast, in Burma, hours of traveling in overcrowded jeeps down forest tracks and mountain paths were rewarded by the sight of exquisite landscapes and encounters with some of the most welcoming people in Asia. Similarly in China, although it seemed that every day another complex negotiation was needed to enable us to continue our journey down the Li River; the beauty of the mountainous country compensated for any frustration. We were less fortunate in Laos, where all our attempts to travel beyond the capital were defeated by bureaucracy. But then in Borneo I was granted the ultimate privilege of traveling deep in virgin rain forest, where no human race has ever lived.

Not unexpectedly, of the countries in this chapter, it is Burma, bordering India, whose cuisine is most clearly influenced by the style of its larger neighbor. China can be the hardest of all these countries for a vegetarian to travel through. Its most interesting vegetarian dishes are from Buddhist cooking traditions, which are most easily accessible in the cosmopolitan environment of Hong Kong. Conversely, in Thailand, Malaysia, and Indonesia, it is rarely a problem to find sound vegetarian meals, although a tolerance of (or even a liking for) shrimp paste and fish sauce is a big bonus when it comes to enjoying street food. We have omitted such ingredients from the recipes in this chapter and used soy sauce instead. The complex flavors of all the other ingredients combine to make such exciting tastes that the fish flavors are hardly missed. The ingredients for Southeast Asian cooking are increasingly easy to find in European and North American supermarkets, and often in natural foods stores as well, although it's always worth stocking up on the basics when in a Chinese or Thai shop.

Pages 112–113 **The Huang Shan Mountains**

Right **Fresh vegetables piled high in a vegetable market in Burma**

BURMA

Life for the Burmese has changed since we last traveled there in the 1980s. At that time, Burma offered one of the most fascinating travel experiences in Asia. The complications of seven-day visas, closed areas, and unreliable transport were insignificant compared to the visual and cultural treats of a land so steeped in tradition and isolated from the outside. The floodplain of the Irrawaddy River at Pagan dotted with ancient pagodas; the leg-rowing fishermen of Ingle Lake; the giant reclining Buddha of Pegu; the golden spires of the Shwe Dagon pagoda; the morning mists over Rangoon harbor — all were the stuff of lifelong memories.

And the food wasn't bad, either. We ate dishes such as vegetables stir-fried with tamarind; cucumber and toasted-sesame-seed salads; and lemongrass rice. One day, we would love to go back to Burma and see how much of the beauty we enjoyed so much has survived. Until then, we have to make do with the memories and the food.

Shadowy boat traffic
haunts Rangoon harbor
at dawn

CUCUMBER AND SESAME SEED SALAD

SERVES 4–6

1 heaping tablespoon sesame seeds
1 tablespoon sunflower oil
2 red onions, thinly sliced
2 garlic cloves
1 large cucumber, peeled and diced

Dressing
2 tablespoons cider vinegar
½ teaspoon ground turmeric
1 generous teaspoon packed brown
   sugar or honey
2 tablespoons Asian sesame oil
Salt to taste

Toast the sesame seeds in a small skillet until they start to pop, then set aside. Heat the sunflower oil in a skillet over medium heat and sauté the onions and garlic until caramelized and brown.

Make the dressing by slowly mixing the vinegar with the turmeric and sugar or honey, then stir in the sesame oil. Season with salt.

Pour the dressing over the diced cucumber and top with the fried onions and garlic and toasted sesame seeds.

LEMONGRASS RICE

Serves 4–6

1 small red onion, coarsely chopped

2 garlic cloves

2 fresh red Thai or serrano chilies, coarsely chopped

2 cups basmati rice

Water as needed

Salt to taste

2 lemongrass stalks (white part only), cut down the middle and crushed with a rolling pin

Juice of 1 lime

Process the onion, garlic, and chilies in a food processor until a paste forms.

Rinse the rice until the water turns clear. Put it in a saucepan with a tight-fitting lid and add enough water to cover by ½ inch. Add salt and the lemongrass and bring to a boil. Cover, reduce the heat, and simmer until all the water is absorbed. Fluff the rice with a fork, at the same time stirring in the onion paste. Cook over very low heat for 5 minutes. Squeeze over the lime juice and adjust the seasoning.

STIR-FRY WITH TAMARIND GRAVY

SERVES 4–6

1 red onion, coarsely chopped

3 garlic cloves

3 fresh red Thai or serrano chilies

1-inch piece fresh ginger, peeled and coarsely chopped

2 lemongrass stalks (white part only), thinly sliced

2 teaspoons cumin seeds, toasted and ground

1 teaspoon dark soy sauce or shrimp paste

2 tablespoons tamarind paste

1 cup hot water

3 tablespoons sunflower oil

1 bunch green onions, cut into ¼-inch slices

2 carrots, peeled and cut into matchsticks

1 pound napa cabbage, cut into 1-inch strips

10 ounces bok choy, coarsely cut

8 ounces thin asparagus, cut into 3-inch pieces

2 red bell peppers, seeded, deribbed, and thinly sliced

2 teaspoons packed brown sugar or honey

2 tablespoons light soy sauce (optional)

Salt to taste

Garnish

Large handful of fresh cilantro leaves, chopped

Large handful of bean sprouts

In a food processor, process the red onion, garlic, chilies, ginger, lemongrass, cumin, and dark soy sauce or shrimp paste until a paste forms. Dissolve the tamarind paste in the hot water.

In a wok over high heat, heat the sunflower oil and stir-fry the onion paste for a few seconds. Add the green onions, carrots, napa cabbage, bok choy, asparagus, and bell peppers. Stir-fry until the vegetables are all coated in the paste and start to soften. Gradually add the tamarind water a little at a time until the vegetables are just cooked.

Add the brown sugar or honey, optional soy sauce, and salt. Garnish with cilantro and bean sprouts piled on top of the dish.

Pagan, on the floodplain of the Irrawaddy River, is like a setting for a fairy tale. Majestic temple ruins in their hundreds are scattered over the plains along the meandering river. When we were there, only the most basic accommodation was available. After a long, hot, dusty day's cycling around the ruins, we really enjoyed the Stir-Fry with Tamarind Gravy served by the family who ran our rustic guesthouse.

After dinner, the women of the house offered us a local-style massage, which involved their walking over our backs with animated vigor. They giggled so much as they did this that we half-suspected it to be a joke they played on passing foreigners.

Stir-Fry with Tamarind Gravy

CHINA

Our one experience of China was a boat journey down the Li Xian and Pearl rivers from Yangshuo to the South China Sea at Hong Kong — perhaps one of the most beautiful river journeys in the world. The Huang Shan Mountains around Yangshuo form the round-topped, sheer-sided shapes familiar from classical Chinese paintings. One night, we slept in a cave near the summit of one of the hills so that we could photograph the dawn mists rising through the extraordinary landscape. During the day, we hired bicycles to explore the rice paddies and villages between the peaks.

Southern China is a bit of a horror show for vegetarians. Most villages we stopped in had drab cafés where surly waiters threw frightening bowls of gruel down on dirty tables. Sometimes the "menu" was a stack of cages stuffed with all kinds of animals, including rats, cats, and owls. Some days we lived off boiled rice and raw peanuts.

We were relieved to get back to Hong Kong, one of the world's most interesting cities in which to discover unusual food. Some dishes use extraordinary ingredients such as tree moss and fermented gluten, while others are simple but enticing combinations of mushrooms or mixed vegetables in light sauces.

A rice paddy near Yangshuo

"BUDDHIST MEAT" AND SHIITAKE MUSHROOMS

Several of Hong Kong's islands offer an almost rural escape from the intensity of the city. Lantau is not the quietest, but it is one of the most rewarding to visit. There is a good walk up to the hilltop monastery of Po Lin, where the monks invite visitors to eat lunch with them; it was at Po Lin that I first ate this dish of "Buddhist meat" with shiitake mushrooms.

"Buddhist meat" is the popular name for seitan, or wheat gluten, which can be found in natural foods stores and Chinese shops. If there is a problem getting hold of seitan, tofu can be used instead; the dry pre-fried style works best, but firm tofu can be used.

SERVES 4

5 tablespoons sunflower oil

1-inch piece fresh ginger, peeled and thinly sliced

3 garlic cloves, thinly sliced

8 ounces shiitake mushrooms, stemmed and quartered

4 carrots, peeled and cut into matchsticks

1 bunch green onions, cut into 1-inch pieces

Salt to taste

10 ounces seitan or fried tofu, cut into strips

1 tablespoon hoisin sauce

1 tablespoon light soy sauce

1 tablespoon shaoxing (rice wine)

1 teaspoon Asian sesame oil

Pepper to taste

¼ cup water

Toasted sesame seeds for garnish

Heat 3 tablespoons of the sunflower oil in a wok over high heat and stir-fry half the ginger and half the garlic for about 20 seconds. Add the mushrooms, carrots, and most of the green onions and toss in the hot oil for 2 minutes. Remove these vegetables, sprinkle them with salt, and set aside.

Wipe out the wok. Heat the remaining oil over high heat and stir-fry the seitan or tofu with the remaining garlic and ginger until it begins to brown.

Combine the hoisin sauce, soy sauce, wine, sesame oil, and a little salt and pepper in a bowl with the water, then pour into the wok. Return the vegetables to the wok and simmer gently for a few minutes.

Serve with steamed rice, and garnish with the rest of the green onions and the sesame seeds.

SOUTH CHINA STIR-FRY

This is a simple, healthy, clean-tasting combination of fresh vegetables cooked quickly in a little oil and flavored with fresh ginger and rice wine. Any vegetables can be used.

SERVES 4–6

4 ounces asparagus

4 ounces cauliflower florets

1 cup broccoli florets

4 tablespoons sunflower oil

3-inch piece fresh ginger, cut into matchsticks

2 ounces shiitake mushrooms, stemmed

8 ounces straw mushrooms, drained

4 ounces sugar snap peas

4 ounces baby corn ears, cut in half lengthwise

4 fresh Thai or serrano red chilies, cut into strips

2 teaspoons cornstarch, mixed to a paste with a little water

2 tablespoons rice wine

2 tablespoons soy sauce

1 teaspoon salt

1 teaspoon sugar

Finely chopped green onions for garnish

Cook the asparagus, cauliflower, and broccoli in salted boiling water for 1 minute, then plunge them into cold water and drain.

Heat the oil in a large wok over high heat until smoking, then add the ginger, all the vegetables, and the chilies. Stir-fry for 5 minutes.

Stir in all the remaining ingredients except the garnish. Serve garnished with green onions and accompanied with rice.

In southern China, we were "slightly" arrested for being slightly off limits. It was a genuine mistake on our part, and a nervous provincial policeman decided that instead of putting us in cells he would invite us to be guests in his home for the night, before sending us back to a town "on limits."

We managed to convey our desire for a meatless meal in time to save any embarrassment during the evening meal with his family. This stir-fry turned out to be the best meal we ate in China. The vegetables are the same ones the policeman's wife had found in the local market that day.

The distinctive peaks of the Huang Shan Mountains towering over a tributary of the Li Xian River near Yangshuo

LAOS

In the late 1980s, Laos began to open up after decades of isolation, and as we were in Thailand anyway, we decided to go and have a look. We especially wanted to visit the temple sites of the first Lao kingdom and the old French colonial mansions in Luang Phabang. The Laotian Embassy in Bangkok refused us visas, but we booked a two-week "package," including visas, through a scruffy little tourist agency. We crossed the Mekong on a small ferry at dawn. The immigration officers seemed happy with our visas, which, written in Lao script, meant nothing to us, and we struck up an acquaintance with a couple returning to Laos for the first time since escaping as refugees

Detail from a Buddhist temple in Vientiane

We first ate this stir-fry on the banks of the mighty Mekong River, at the village wedding feast we had been invited to by our new friends. The thickening of puréed eggplants is characteristic of Laotian dishes – eggplants are abundant in Laos.

fifteen years before. They were on their way to a village near Vientiane, the capital, for a family wedding, and with typical Asian hospitality they invited us to accompany them. We spent several enjoyable hours at the feast, sharing in the double celebration of the reunion and the wedding festivities, and eating vast quantities of delicious food.

That was the good bit. The next day, having reluctantly spent a night in our somber prepaid hotel in Vientiane, a compulsory part of the package, we tried to organize a flight or a boat journey to Luang Phabang, only to find, to our dismay, that our visas were good only for Vientiane and, moreover, expired that day. We had no option but to return to the ferry. And that was all we saw of Laos.

MEKONG STIR-FRY WITH PUREED EGGPLANT

Serves 4–6

2 large Japanese eggplants
3 tablespoons sunflower oil
6 green onions, cut into ¼-inch slices
3 garlic cloves, crushed
3 fresh red Thai or serrano chilies, thinly sliced
1 teaspoon fennel seeds, crushed
8 ounces shiitake mushrooms, stemmed and thickly sliced
8 ounces baby green beans, cut in half crosswise
½ bunch spinach, stemmed and shredded
8 ounces sugar snap peas
2-inch piece galangal or ginger, peeled and thinly sliced
Water as needed
Handful of fresh mint leaves
Handful of fresh basil leaves
Salt to taste

Cut off the top of the eggplants and slice the rest in half lengthwise. Immerse in a saucepan of salted boiling water and simmer until the flesh is soft. Remove from the pan and scoop the flesh from the skin using a spoon. Either mash the flesh using a potato masher or purée in a food processor. Set aside.

Heat the oil in a wok over high heat and stir-fry the green onions, garlic, and chilies. Add the fennel seeds, then the mushrooms and green beans, and stir-fry for 1 or 2 minutes. Add the spinach and sugar snap peas, stirring constantly. Add the eggplant purée, galangal or ginger, and enough water to make a sauce. Simmer until the vegetables are just cooked. Stir in the mint, basil, and salt. Serve with noodles and Crunchy Sweet-and-Sour Salad (page 126).

CRUNCHY SWEET-AND-SOUR SALAD

SERVES 4–6

⅓ small head of napa cabbage, thinly
   sliced

1 bunch watercress, stemmed

Large handful of spinach leaves,
   stemmed and sliced

8 ounces bean sprouts

3 ounces snow peas, cut into strips
   lengthwise

Dressing

2 tablespoons canola oil

3 garlic cloves, sliced

2 tablespoons fresh lime juice

2 tablespoons light soy sauce

2 teaspoons packed brown sugar or
   honey

2 red Thai or serrano chilies, thinly
   sliced

4 green onions, cut into strips

¾ cup skinned shelled peanuts,
   toasted in a pan and crushed

Small handful of fresh mint

Small handful of basil leaves

Crunchy Sweet-and-Sour Salad is another of the dishes we sampled at the wedding, sitting on the floor among a hundred happy people, with most of whom we didn't share a word of language.

Mix the cabbage, watercress, spinach, bean sprouts, and snow peas in a bowl. To make the dressing: In a small, heavy saucepan over medium heat, heat the oil and fry the garlic until brown and crunchy. Remove the pan from heat and add the lime juice, soy sauce, brown sugar or honey, and the chilies. Stir until all the ingredients are combined. Let cool slightly, then pour over the salad. Sprinkle the green onions, peanuts, and herbs on top.

Left **Detail from a Buddhist temple in Vientiane**

Right **Crunchy Sweet-and-Sour Salad**

THAILAND

Thailand is one of the easy countries of Asia for foreign tourists. It has an abundance of natural beauty, from the jungly hills of the north to the forests and rivers of the center and the tropical paradises of the southern peninsula. Visitors can explore the spectacular ruins of past Siamese kingdoms and colorful living temples, ride an elephant or trek to a tribal village in the hills, and enjoy idyllic beaches, bargain shopping, great-value accommodations and efficient public transport. The country has developed a massive tourist industry, the downside of which is that it is all too easy to spend a trip almost entirely in the company of other tourists. Thailand demands so little in return for all it offers that traveling there almost seems like cheating.

Despite providing such a generous holiday destination, Thais have kept much of the traditional grace and elegance of their way of life, together with a unique cuisine. Never having been invaded or colonized (a singular history in southern Asia), they have food that is undiluted Thai and very good. Fresh ingredients are cooked in heavily spiced pastes and flavored with lemongrass, lime leaves, galangal, black pepper, basil, ginger, tamarind, coconut milk, peanuts, and cilantro. Being completely vegetarian can be complicated by the fish and shrimp sauces that are much used in Thai cooking, but these can easily be excluded when cooking at home. Anyone who enjoys eating fish and seafood will be well satisfied, especially in southern Thailand. There are some excellent vegetarian restaurants in Bangkok and in larger towns such as Chiang Mai. Some are smart and relatively expensive; others, including those set up by the Theravada Buddhists, indicated by a large green sign with a Thai numeral on it, are incredibly cheap.

One of our first experiences of travel in Asia was several weeks spent living for a few pence a night in palm-thatched beach huts on various islands in the Gulf of Thailand. Our budget was so tight that we didn't want to use any of it buying the food on sale in the tourist cafés along the beach, so we cooked every night on a paraffin stove outside our hut, using whatever we found in the local market. We didn't know much about Thai cooking at the time, but simply enjoyed experimenting with all the ingredients we came across. Since then, we have learned far more about how to use these ingredients to create more traditional and much tastier Thai dishes.

A huge statue of the Buddha in the ruins of Sukhothai, the ancient Siamese capital

This stir-fry is a dish we ate on the street in Bangkok after watching a film in an open-air street cinema. The film was projected onto a sheet suspended between two trees. It cost a few *bhat* to sit in front of the trees, while to watch the film back to front behind the sheet was free. Both sides of the sheet drew large crowds, as did the street-food stalls, which produced this feast in just a few minutes.

BANGKOK STIR-FRY

SERVES 4

- 4 tablespoons sunflower oil
- 8 Japanese eggplants, cut into 1-inch pieces
- Salt to taste
- 10 ounces deep-fried tofu, cut into ½-inch slices
- 8 ounces green beans, cut into 2-inch pieces
- 4 fresh red Thai or serrano chilies, cut into strips
- Good pinch of red pepper flakes
- 2 teaspoons packed brown sugar
- 1¾ cups (14 ounces) coconut milk
- Handful of chopped fresh cilantro leaves for garnish

Make sure you have all ingredients prepared and at hand.

Heat the sunflower oil in a wok over high heat and stir-fry the eggplant, sprinkled with a little salt to keep it from absorbing too much oil and drying out, until it starts to soften. Add the tofu and green beans and stir-fry for a few minutes. Add the chilies, the pepper flakes, and brown sugar, stirring constantly.

Reduce the heat and add the coconut milk. Simmer for 5 minutes. Season with salt to taste. Serve with noodles, garnished with cilantro.

JUNGLE CURRY

This curry is made with a red curry paste that can be made in advance and stored in the refrigerator.

SERVES 4–6

Red Curry Paste

4 fresh red Thai or serrano chilies

4 garlic cloves

2 lemongrass stalks (white part only), thinly sliced

2-inch cube fresh galangal or ginger, peeled and chopped

1 red onion, coarsely chopped

½ teaspoon salt

2 teaspoons coriander seeds, toasted and ground

4 tablespoons sunflower oil

5 ounces baby corn ears, cut down the middle lengthwise

2 small red bell peppers, seeded, deribbed and thinly sliced

8 ounces green beans, cut in half

8 ounces button mushrooms, cut in half

2 small heads broccoli, broken into florets

1½ cups vegetable stock

1 tablespoon dark soy sauce

4 kaffir lime leaves, rolled and thinly sliced

2 teaspoons packed brown sugar

Salt to taste

Garnish

Chopped fresh cilantro

Fresh red Thai or serrano chilies, thinly sliced

Make the red curry paste by processing all the ingredients together in a food processor.

Heat the sunflower oil in a wok over high heat and fry the red curry paste for a few seconds, stirring constantly. Add the vegetables and stir-fry until they are well coated with the paste and starting to soften.

Pour over the stock and soy sauce. Add the lime leaves and sugar. Simmer until the vegetables are crisp-tender, adding water if necessary.

Add salt. Garnish with cilantro and chilies. Serve with rice or noodles and Spicy Bean Curd and Bean Sprout Salad (page 133).

"Jungle curries," from the northern part of Thailand, are characterized by strong flavors and the absence of the sweet coconut milk so favored in the south. The most memorable jungle curry we tasted was one that we ate while staying in a forest guest house among the great Buddha statues that are scattered around the ruins of Sukhothai.

Jungle Curry

THAI GREEN CURRY

SERVES 4–6

4 tablespoons sunflower oil

6 Japanese eggplants, cut into 1-inch
  pieces, or 8 Thai eggplants, cut in
  half

⅔ head cauliflower, cut into small
  florets

5 ounces green beans, cut in half

6 ounces oyster mushrooms, sliced

⅓ cup vegetable stock

4 kaffir lime leaves, rolled up and
  thinly sliced

4 teaspoons dark soy sauce

2 teaoons packed brown sugar

1¼ cups coconut milk

Large handful of fresh basil leaves

Salt to taste

Chopped fresh cilantro, for garnish

Green Curry Paste

1 teaspoon coriander seeds

1 teaspoon cumin seeds

2 teaspoons black peppercorns

Large handful of fresh cilantro
  stems, chopped

6 shallots or 1 red onion, coarsely
  chopped

4 garlic cloves

2-inch cube fresh galangal or ginger,
  peeled and coarsely chopped

2 lemongrass stalks (white part
  only), thinly sliced

4 fresh green Thai or serrano chilies

1 tablespoon dark soy sauce or
  1 teaspoon fish sauce

Grated zest and juice of 1 lime

Thai Green Curry, with its aromatic coconut milk sauce, is typical of the south, and is our favorite Thai curry. It is actually not very green, but most of the ingredients of the paste that forms the basis of the curry are. You can use almost any vegetable, but eggplant works particularly well. If you can get small round Thai eggplants, all the better; Japanese eggplants are a good substitute and are available in most good supermarkets.

To make the green curry paste: Toast the coriander and cumin seeds in a small pan, then mix them with the peppercorns and grind, using a spice grinder or pestle and mortar. Add to a food processor with all the remaining curry ingredients and process until a paste forms. Store in the refrigerator if making in advance.

Heat the sunflower oil in a wok over high heat and stir-fry the eggplants (sprinkled with a little salt to prevent them absorbing all the oil and drying up too much) until they start to soften. Add the cauliflower, green beans, and oyster mushrooms.

When the cauliflower starts to brown, add the green curry paste, stirring well to avoid sticking. Add the stock, kaffir lime leaves, soy sauce, and sugar. When the vegetables are just starting to soften, reduce heat and add the coconut milk and basil. Cook for 5 minutes, making sure that the sauce doesn't boil. Season with salt. Serve with rice or noodles, garnished with chopped cilantro.

Fried bean curd (tofu) makes a lovely side dish to serve with any of the Thai curries in this chapter. Deep-fried tofu can be bought from any natural foods store or Asian market, or from good supermarkets, which is much easier than frying it yourself.

The Buddha's hand — a detail from one of the statues around the ruins of Sukhothai

SPICY BEAN CURD AND BEAN SPROUT SALAD

SERVES 4–6

1 cucumber, grated

1 red bell pepper, seeded, deribbed, and cut into fine strips

8 ounces bean sprouts

1 tablespoon sunflower oil

10 ounces deep-fried tofu, cut into ½-inch slices

1 garlic clove, crushed

1–2 fresh green Thai or serrano chilies, thinly sliced

1–2 fresh red Thai or serrano chilies, thinly sliced

Juice of 1 lime

2 tablespoons light soy sauce

2 teapoons packed brown sugar or honey

¾ cup skinned peanuts, toasted in a pan and crushed

Handful of fresh cilantro leaves, chopped

Combine the grated cucumber, bell pepper, and bean sprouts in a salad bowl.

Heat the oil in a skillet over medium heat and fry the tofu slices until they are brown and crunchy. Set aside and let cool.

Using the same pan, sauté the garlic and chilies for a few seconds, then add the lime juice, soy sauce, and brown sugar or honey. Stir until all these dressing ingredients are combined.

Arrange the fried tofu slices on top of the salad and sprinkle with the crushed peanuts. Pour on the hot dressing and garnish with lots of cilantro.

MALAYSIA & INDONESIA

Peninsular Malaysia, Borneo, and all the Indonesian islands share an essentially common language and cuisine. The language, Bahasa, is very easy to learn, and with little variation the spoken language is understood all the way from the air-conditioned office blocks of Kuala Lumpur and Jakarta to the most remote longhouse in the jungles of Sarawak or Irian Jaya. Numerous regional languages, Chinese dialects, and Tamil are spoken through the region, but a knowledge of Bahasa will enable a tourist to communicate with most people, most of the time.

As far as food is concerned, there are regional variations too, and rather more of a difference between Malaysia and Indonesia than with language. The ingredients themselves remain more constant. Vegetarian food is easy to find. A street-food classic is the delicious satay sauce, made from roasted peanuts blended with spices, into which grilled chicken or red meat is usually dipped. Luckily for vegetarians, a raw vegetable and bean curd dish, *gado gado* (page 143), served with a similar sauce, is common throughout Indonesia. There are also numerous fried rice, bean curd, and egg dishes, as well as vegetable concoctions in coconut milk curries, to choose from.

Peninsular Malaysia, like Thailand, is so undemanding of the tourist that it makes for a perfect holiday destination. The east coast is less developed than the richer, more urban west; some of the offshore islands are sensationally beautiful, and a train journey from Gemas to Kota Bharu through the center passes through some impressive rain forests. My real jungle experience came on a Royal Geographical Society assignment to the Batu Apoi Forest Reserve, in the remote Temburong district of eastern Brunei on the island of Borneo. Thanks to its phenomenal oil wealth, Brunei's tropical rain forests have largely escaped being cut for profit. In this, as in much else, it differs sharply from the rest of Borneo.

To reach the reserve, I had to travel from the capital, down the Brunei River, across open sea, through mangrove swamps, and up the Temburong River to the sleepy settlement of Bangar. A Land Rover then took me cross-country to an Iban longhouse at Batang Duri on the Kuala (River) Belalong. From here the journey was by motorized canoe, negotiating rocks and rapids all the way up to the riverside jungle clearing, where a collection of wooden huts on stilts was to be my home for the next six weeks.

A highlight of my trip was a four-day trek to Bukit Belalong, the topmost point in the reserve. Sleeping out in the forest on stretchers suspended above the forest floor, so as to escape the worst of the leeches, was much more cozy than I had imagined it

The dense rain forest of the remote Batu Apoi Forest Reserve

would be. Bed was the only place to be dry, and we carefully preserved a spare set of dry clothes to sleep in, changing back into our damp daytime clothing in the morning. There was no point in trying to stay dry: Within seconds of setting off into the forest, perspiration and dampness from the regular rainfall soaked everything. Putting on wet clothes isn't the most pleasant way to start a day — but the dawn chorus of gibbon calls above the mutterings of a million birds and insects made up for a lot. In fact, I have found that one way of conveying how amazing it is to be in the rain forest is to first relate the hardships — which include constant thirst, complete exhaustion, fear of getting lost (and dying), sliding painfully down steep muddy banks, and finding leeches in one's underclothes. For, despite all this, it is still an unforgettable experience in an entirely positive way.

SPICY GARLIC-FRIED GREEN VEGETABLES

Black bean paste, made from soybeans, is available at most supermarkets or Asian groceries; if you can't find it, use finely chopped salted black soybeans.

SERVES 4–6

- 4 tablespoons sunflower oil
- 8 shallots or 2 red onions, thinly sliced
- 4 garlic cloves, sliced
- 4 fresh red Thai or serrano chilies, thinly sliced
- 4 small zucchini, cut into ¼-inch-thick matchsticks
- 5 ounces okra, cut in half lengthwise
- 8 ounces sugar snap peas
- 1 small head of napa cabbage, cut into 1-inch slices
- 8 ounces spinach, stemmed and shredded
- 2 tablespoons black bean paste, or 1 tablespoon salted black soybeans, minced and mixed with 1 tablespoon water
- 2 tablespoons packed brown sugar or honey
- 2 tablespoons dark soy sauce
- 5 tablespoons water

Heat the oil in a wok over high heat and stir-fry the shallots or onions, garlic, and chilies for 2 minutes.

Add the zucchini, okra, sugar snap peas, and cabbage, and stir-fry until the vegetables start to soften. Add the spinach and stir-fry until it starts to wilt. Add the black bean paste or minced black bean mixture, brown sugar or honey, and soy sauce. Stir well.

Add the water and stir-fry until all the ingredients are well combined. Serve immediately.

We watched these spicy garlic-fried green vegetables being cooked in front of our eyes at a stall in a Singapore food market. As with most stir-fries, the recipe relies on a hot wok and all the ingredients being at hand ready to add. This can be served as a side dish or as a main course.

MALAYSIAN FRUIT AND VEGETABLE SALAD

SERVES 4–6

1 small firm mango, peeled, cut
   from the pit, and cubed
1 firm pear, peeled, cored, and
   cubed
½ pineapple, peeled, cored, and
   cubed
2 carrots, peeled and cubed
4 ounces bean sprouts
1 red bell pepper, seeded, deribbed,
   and cut into thin slices

Dressing
2 tablespoons light soy sauce

2 tablespoons water
2 teaspoons honey or packed brown
   sugar
1 fresh red Thai or serrano chili,
   minced
1 tablespoon tamarind paste
Juice of 1 lime

Garnish
1 tablespoon crushed toasted
   skinned peanuts
Handful of fresh cilantro leaves,
   chopped

Combine all the fruits and vegetables in a salad bowl.

Combine all the dressing ingredients and stir until the sugar has dissolved.

Pour the dressing over the salad. Sprinkle with crushed peanuts and chopped cilantro leaves to serve.

MALAY SAMBAL

SERVES 4—6

2 small red onions, coarsely
  chopped
4 garlic cloves
4 fresh red Thai or serrano chilies
½ cup ground almonds
2 lemongrass stalks (white part
  only), thinly sliced
2-inch cube fresh galangal or ginger,
  peeled and chopped
2 tomatoes, coarsely chopped
4 tablespoons sunflower oil
2 sweet potatoes, peeled and cubed
4 carrots, peeled and cut into
  matchsticks
½ small white cabbage, cored and
  finely shredded
7 ounces baby corn ears, halved
  lengthwise
1 bunch green onions, cut into
  1-inch strips

4 kaffir lime leaves, rolled up and
  thinly sliced
Water as needed
1 cup coconut milk
2 teaspoons sugar or honey
Juice of 1 lime
Salt to taste

Garnish
4 ounces bean sprouts
⅓ cucumber, grated
2 fresh red Thai or serrano chilies,
  thinly sliced lengthwise
Handful of fresh cilantro leaves,
  chopped
Good shake of soy sauce
Juice of 1 lime
⅓ cup crushed roasted peanuts

The island of Tioman on
Malaysia's east coast can
be reached by fishing
boat from Mersing. From
the jetty, a footpath
climbs into the rain
forest, past giant monitor
lizards and waterfalls,
over a ridge, then steeply
down to the refreshingly
clear water of the South
China Sea at Kampung
Juara. We stayed here,
sleeping a few yards
from the sea in a simple
A-frame hut and eating
each day in one of the
two beach cafés, where
we discovered the Malay
sambal dish that we
describe here.

In a food processor, process the red onions, garlic, chilies, almonds, lemongrass,
galangal or ginger, and tomatoes together. Set aside.

Heat the sunflower oil in a wok over high heat and stir-fry the sweet potatoes
until they start to brown. Add the carrots and stir-fry for a few minutes. Then
add the cabbage and stir-fry until it starts to wilt. Add the corn, green onions,
lime leaves, and tomato mixture. Stir until the vegetables are coated. Add
enough water to make a thick sauce and gently simmer until the vegetables are
crisp-tender. Add the coconut milk, sugar or honey, lime juice, and salt. Simmer
for 1 or 2 minutes.

Combine all the garnish ingredients. Serve the *sambal* with rice, sprinkled
with the garnish mixture.

KUCHING TAMARIND AND COCONUT MILK CURRY

This curry, which is very popular across southern Malaysia and Kuching, is particularly good with noodles.

SERVES 4 6

1 red onion or 6 shallots, coarsely
   chopped

3 garlic cloves

4 fresh red Thai or serrano chilies

2 teaspoons tamarind paste

1 tablespoon dark soy sauce

Scant ½ teaspoon ground turmeric

4 tablespoons sunflower oil

6 Japanese eggplants, cut into 1-inch
   pieces

Salt to taste

½ small white cabbage, cored and
   finely shredded

1 large red bell pepper, seeded,
   deribbed, and thinly sliced

Water as needed

10 ounces bok choy, coarsely
   chopped

1¾ cups (14 ounces) coconut milk

8 ounces bean sprouts

Garnish

2 shallots, thinly sliced

Large handful of fresh cilantro
   leaves, chopped

2 fresh red Thai or serrano chilies,
   thinly sliced

Chinese characters on a
shop front in Malaysia

Puree the onion or shallots, garlic, chilies, tamarind paste, soy sauce, and turmeric together in a food processor until they form a paste.

Heat the sunflower oil in a wok over high heat and stir-fry the eggplants, sprinkled with a little salt to prevent it from absorbing too much oil.

Add the flavoring paste and stir well until the eggplant is coated with it. Add the cabbage and bell pepper, stirring constantly. Add some water to loosen the spices and make a sauce. Cook until the vegetables are crisp-tender.

Add the bok choy, coconut milk, and bean sprouts. Simmer for 3 minutes, but do not boil. If necessary, add salt to taste.

Serve in bowls with a generous garnish of shallots, chopped cilantro, and chilies.

BORNEO RAIN FOREST VEGETABLES

SERVES 4–6

1 teaspoon ground coriander
1 teaspoon red pepper flakes
1 teaspoon ground turmeric
2 teaspoons ground almonds
1 large onion
4 garlic cloves
3 tablespoons sunflower oil
10 ounces tempeh, cut into strips
3 tablespoons cashew nuts
1 lemongrass stalk (white part only), cut into short lengths and crushed
2-inch piece fresh galangal or ginger, chopped and crushed

7 ounces baby corn ears, halved lengthwise
1 cup cauliflower florets
8 ounces green beans, cut in half lengthwise
1¼ cups (14 ounces) coconut milk
1 tablespoon coconut milk powder, mixed to a paste with water

Garnish
Thin strips of fresh red Thai or serrano chili
Fresh cilantro leaves
Roasted peanuts

In a food processor, puree the coriander, pepper flakes, turmeric, almonds, onion, and garlic to a paste.

Heat the oil in a heavy saucepan over medium heat and sauté the tempeh and cashew nuts until they turn brown. Add the garlic paste, lemongrass, and galangal or ginger, and cook for 2 minutes.

Add all the vegetables and toss to coat in the paste. Add the coconut milk and simmer until the vegetables are tender.

Remove the lemongrass and galangal, or ginger, and stir in the coconut milk paste to thicken.

Serve with rice, garnished with red chili, cilantro leaves, and peanuts.

One of the most pleasant surprises during my stay at the Batu Apoi Forest Reserve in Brunei was the presence of two excellent and entertaining Indonesian cooks; another was the location of an Iban "short house" on the edge of the camp to accommodate the Iban guides and porters. Between cooking and language lessons and Iban hospitality, there was never a dull evening. By day the rain forest, awesome in its scale and mystery, provided countless photographic delights and a feeling of complete disregard for anything that might exist beyond it. This tempeh and cashew-nut dish that I ate there is one of the best reminders of that time.

Borneo Rain Forest Vegetables

We loved Bali; the food was excellent, the people graceful and friendly, the temples fascinating, and the landscapes enchanting. It was refreshing to see a place where mass tourism has been managed so well, maintaining most of the dignity and traditions of the local culture while providing comfortable accommodations and such good food for visitors. We did not see the whole island, and there may well be places where this equation has not been so convincing, but for us, Bali was traveling at its best.

Our favorite beach-side lunch in Bali, *gado gado*, is an unusual combination of hot and cold ingredients. The cooked peanut sauce is poured over a crunchy salad, which is served with hard-boiled eggs and dry-fried onions.

Balinese Gado Gado

BALINESE GADO GADO

Serves 4–6

Peanut sauce

1 large red onion, coarsely chopped

3 garlic cloves

3 fresh red Thai or serrano chilies

6 ounces skinned peanuts

2 tablespoons sunflower oil

1 tablespoon soy sauce

2 teaspoons tamarind paste, dissolved in 2 tablespoons water

⅓ cup coconut milk

1 tablespoon smooth peanut butter

2 teaspoons packed brown sugar

2 lemongrass stalks (white part only), cut down the middle and crushed

Water as needed

Salt to taste

3 carrots, peeled and cut into matchsticks

8 ounces bean sprouts

4 ounces green beans

4 ounces sugar snap peas

½ cucumber, cut into ¼-inch-wide matchsticks

1 small head of napa cabbage, thinly sliced

Garnish

4 hard-boiled eggs, cut into wedges

4 tomatoes, cut into wedges

8 ounces tempeh, cut into strips and fried, or ½-inch slices deep-fried tofu, fried until crunchy

Large handful of stemmed spinach leaves, shredded

1 large onion, dry-fried (page 145)

Handful of fresh cilantro leaves, chopped

To make the sauce: Puree the onion, garlic, and chilies together in a food processor until they form a paste. Toast the peanuts in a pan, stirring to avoid burning. Let cool and process in a food processor until finely ground.

Heat the oil in a wok over high heat and fry the onion paste, stirring constantly, for 1 minute. Add the ground peanuts and stir until all the ingredients are combined. Add the soy sauce, tamarind mixture, coconut milk, peanut butter, sugar, and lemongrass. Gently cook until all the flavors are combined and a thick sauce has formed (add a little water if necessary). Remove the lemongrass and season the sauce with salt.

Combine all the vegetables (you can serve this dish either in individual portions or in one big bowl). Pour the warm sauce over the salad, then arrange the eggs, tomatoes, and tempeh or tofu around the edge and pile the spinach and dry-fried onions in the center. Sprinkle with cilantro.

TEMPEH GORENG AND BEAN SPROUTS

SERVES 4–6

4 garlic cloves, crushed

1 teaspoon ground coriander

2 tablepoons water

4 tablespoons sunflower oil

8 ounces tempeh, cut into chunky
   sticks

8 ounces bean sprouts

3 tablespoons soy sauce

Mix the crushed garlic and coriander with the water to make a paste.

Heat the oil in a skillet over medium heat and sauté the tempeh sticks until
brown, stirring them gently. Add the garlic paste. After 30 seconds, add the bean
sprouts. Mix well, add the soy sauce, and serve.

Tempeh goreng is real
bus-station food. In Bali,
even in small towns, bus
stations encourage fast-
food street stalls. At
night, they are enter-
taining, even romantic
places to eat, all lit up
and full of animated
bustle. By day, however,
the illusion is swiftly
shattered by the number
of flies and the state of
the kitchens.

Left The spectacularly located Tanah Lot shore temple in Bali

Right A typical Malaysian food stall in a Penang street

The thin, spicy sauces known as *sambals* form part of most meals in Malaysia and Indonesia.

Usually a table will be laid with *sambals* and a variety of other accompaniments, all served in small dishes. We list a few suggestions here:

Dry-fried onions (thinly sliced and gently fried in a hot, dry pan until brown)
Thinly sliced red onions
Sliced fresh chilies
Sliced green onions
Crushed roasted peanuts
Sliced cucumber
Grated coconut
Tempeh (broken up into small pieces, then fried in oil until brown)

MALAYSIAN SAMBAL

SERVES 4–6

2 green Thai or serrano chilies, minced
2 fresh red Thai or serrano chilies, minced
2 green onions, finely chopped
½ teaspoon salt
Juice of 1 lime
2 teaspoons honey or packed brown sugar
1 tablespoon cider vinegar

Mix all the ingredients together and let sit for 15 minutes before serving.

INDONESIAN SAMBAL

SERVES 4–6

2 garlic cloves, minced
2 fresh red Thai or serrano chilies, minced
Juice of ½ lime
1 teaspoon sugar or honey
2 tablespoons dark soy sauce

Mix all the ingredients together and let sit for 15 minutes before serving.

The

Americas

Beans and rice are the ubiquitous staples of the cuisines of South and central America and southern North America. In every country we visited between the Rio Grande of Mexico and Rio de Janeiro in Brazil, we ate beans and rice in one form or another. There are many regional variations in the way beans and rice are served, and this chapter includes some of the most delicious. Other dishes — especially vegetarian ones — did sometimes prove rather hard to track down. Brazil and Mexico offered the most interesting variety: Here we found lots of exciting fresh fruits and vegetables and cheeses, with spicy sauces and salsas. In the Andean countries, we were offered stews of corn and squash, while in Costa Rica the beans and rice were punctuated with salads and Caribbean tastes such as plantain and coconut milk. In Cuba, it was sometimes a problem to find anything to eat at all.

To some extent, the cities of South and Central America and southern North America are European in flavor. However, on the outskirts of large cities, shanty towns and *favelas* are swollen by the exodus of rural poor joining the deprived urban underclass. The affluent elite of such cities as Rio, La Paz, Lima, and Quito are more likely to be descended from the colonizers rather than from indigenous South Americans. It is easy (if somewhat expensive) to stay in such cities, eating only in the restaurants of the privileged, and it can be rather dangerous as a

Pages 146–147
Sunset over Rio de
Janeiro

Above A tortilla is
deftly filled with cheese
at a street stall in
Oaxaca, Mexico

Left A woman leads her
llama through the
streets of Cuzco, Peru

foreigner to venture too far from comfortable familiarity into the twilight zones
of raw street life.

Beyond the cities, there are better opportunities to gain experiences of culture and people outside the European traditions. In the rain forests of the
Brazilian Amazon, on the high altiplano of the Andes, and in the coastal deserts
of Peru, we traveled through some stunning landscapes and met plenty of
indigenous people ranging from tribal forest Indians to Quechua-speaking
mountain *campesinos*. However, I'm afraid that in South America all the best
food we discovered was in the comfortable restaurants and homes of the city
elite. Nonetheless, despite their evident European influences, all the recipes we
have chosen owe as much to the original South Americans as to any colonial
roots.

In Central America and southern North America, our experience was notably
different, and some of the best meals we had in Mexico and Costa Rica were in
roadside, beachside, and jungle cafés, far from the comforts of any city.

BRAZIL

The first time I visited Brazil was for a Royal Geographical Society project in the far northeast, on a remote island called Ilha de Maraca. The island, surrounded by tributaries of the Rio Branco, is covered in dense rain forest. Trails were being cut with machetes by local guides to facilitate the team of scientists due to arrive; I was to photograph the environment in its original state before research began. Apart from the trails, dugout canoes provided the only way of getting around. My second trip to the rain forest was less demanding. In the Itatiaia Reserve between Rio de Janeiro and São Paulo, the hilly terrain gives better views of the forest, which reveals itself as full of waterfalls and butterflies, and is much easier to get to.

Brazilians love to eat meat and some restaurants serve nothing else, by the plateful. However, there is no shortage of excellent vegetarian restaurants in most Brazilian cities. Many are open only at lunchtime and serve fixed-price buffet meals, including selections of fresh salads, fruity salsas, and adaptations of traditional dishes. The cosmopolitan nature of Rio has encouraged a more eclectic choice of ingredients than is found anywhere else in South America.

A view of the Amazon jungle in the rain

On my first day in the rain forest, down river with one of the guides in a canoe, we misjudged some rapids and knocked the outboard motor out of action. With twelve miles of uncut jungle between us and the camp, and piranhas in the water, I felt a very long way from home. Eventually, the guide managed to fix the motor with his machete, and we made it back to base, thankful to have avoided a twenty-day hack though the forest.

That night, the wives of the guides cooked a huge pot of stew for everyone in the camp, a version of the dish *cozido* (which usually contains pork and sausages), using mounds of the fresh vegetables that we had brought with us from Boa Vista.

COZIDO

SERVES 4–6

Marinade

2 garlic cloves, crushed

1 teaspoon coriander seeds, crushed

Handful of parsley sprigs, chopped

1 onion, thinly sliced

2 teaspoons balsamic vinegar

3 tablespoons tamari sauce

3 bay leaves

1 tablespoon olive oil

10 ounces seitan or fried tofu, sliced

2 cups cubed pie pumpkin

5 tablespoons olive oil

1 plantain, peeled and cut into ½-inch slices

4 ounces okra, sliced lengthwise

1 onion, thinly sliced

2 garlic cloves, crushed

1 heaped teaspoon coriander seeds, crushed

2 small turnips, cubed

½ white cabbage, cored and cubed

10 ounces yellow summer squash, cut into 1-inch cubes

2 cups cubed sweet potatoes

1 cup vegetable stock

Handful of fresh parsley sprigs, chopped

Salt and pepper to taste

Combine all the marinade ingredients and pour them over the sliced seitan or tofu in a bowl. Let stand for 1 hour. Pour off the marinade, retaining the liquid, and set the seitan or tofu to one side. Meanwhile, cook the pumpkin in salted boiling water until soft. Drain, retaining the pumpkin water. Mash the pumpkin and set aside.

Heat half the oil in a large, heavy saucepan over medium heat and fry the sliced plantain until browned. Remove from pan. Add the marinated seitan or tofu and the okra, and fry until both are browned. Remove from pan. Heat the remaining oil and add the onion and garlic. When these begin to soften, add the crushed coriander seeds. Stir and add the turnips, cabbage, squash, and sweet potatoes. Stir to coat the vegetables in the oil and coriander. Add the stock, 1 cup of the reserved pumpkin water, and the marinade. Simmer until the vegetables are soft.

Stir in the mashed pumpkin, then add the fried seitan or tofu, okra, and plantain. Simmer gently for a few minutes to allow the flavors to infuse. Add the parsley, salt, and pepper to taste. Serve with rice.

BLACK BEAN STEW

SERVES 4–6

1⅓ cups dried black beans, soaked
    overnight in cold water

2 tablespoons olive oil

1 large red onion, diced

4 garlic cloves, crushed

3 fresh red chilies, finely chopped

2 tablespoons butter

1 pound sweet potatoes, peeled and
    cubed

8 ounces turnips, cubed

2 carrots, peeled and cubed

1 red bell pepper, seeded, deribbed.
    and cubed

2 tomatoes, finely diced

½ cup vegetable stock

2 large handfuls of fresh cilantro
    leaves, chopped, plus more to
    garnish

Handful of fresh parsley sprigs,
    finely chopped

2 bay leaves

Salt and pepper to taste

Drain the black beans, place in a saucepan, and cover with water. Bring to a boil, reduce heat to low, cover, and simmer until the beans are tender.

Meanwhile, heat the olive oil over medium heat in a skillet and fry the onion, garlic, and chilies until soft. Remove a third of the black beans and their cooking liquid and add this to the fried onion. Mash the onion and beans with a potato masher until the beans start to break down. Return to the remaining beans and cooking liquid. Melt the butter in a large saucepan over medium heat and fry the sweet potatoes, turnips, carrots, and bell pepper until they start to soften. Add the tomatoes and fry until the tomatoes break down. Add the black beans and their liquid, the stock, cilantro, parsley, and bay leaves. Simmer until the vegetables are soft and the flavors combined. Season with salt and pepper.

MANGO SALSA

SERVES 4–6

1 large ripe mango, peeled and cubed

2 small carrots, peeled and diced

2 celery stalks, diced

1 orange, peeled and cut into cubes

1 fresh green chili, finely chopped

Handful of fresh cilantro leaves, chopped

Juice of 1 lime

Pepper to taste

Combine all the ingredients and refrigerate for 30 minutes before serving.

This colorful black bean recipe is an adaptation of a traditional Brazilian dish. When served with Mango Salsa, the bright reds and yellows contrast strikingly with the black beans.

Black Bean Stew

BOLIVIA

La Paz is the highest capital city in the world, and my arrival there was a dramatic one. By a twist of fate, having nearly missed the flight from Santa Cruz, I had been invited to fly in the last remaining seat — in the cockpit with the pilot. The view of the Andes rising out of the Amazon Basin, as seen through the windscreen of a 737, was an incredible novelty. As the airplane passed over the snowy peaks in the half-light of dusk, they seemed only a few hundred feet below us; beyond them, La Paz came into view, a bowl of lights sunk in the dark expanse of the altiplano. We descended through

Shadowy figures in the La Paz fog

shafts of lightning from an electrical storm to a runway 12,000 feet above sea level. The air is cold and thin at this altitude. The effort of carrying my bags up to a third-floor hotel room was exhausting and my sleep full of nightmares.

Bolivia was in the midst of its own nightmare, an economic one. Inflation was running at 45,000 percent. The exchange rate for U.S. dollars rose daily, the banks were closed, and on street corners men in leather jackets exchanged pesos by the carrier bag from tea chests full of notes. A cup of coffee cost two million pesos; eating out meant taking along a bag of money to pay the bill. For the first time in my life, I was a millionaire. La Paz was a city of millionaires, many of them desperately poor.

CORN STEW

SERVES 4–6

3 carrots, peeled and diced

3 potatoes, peeled and diced

4 tablespoons sunflower oil

2 onions, finely chopped

4 garlic cloves, crushed

1 jalapeño chili, finely chopped

2 large, ripe plum tomatoes, cubed

1 tablespoon sweet paprika

Leaves from 1 handful fresh oregano, minced

Handful of fresh parsley sprigs, chopped

3 large handfuls of spinach, stemmed and finely shredded

4 ears fresh corn, cut into rounds 1-inch-thick and blanched

2 cups vegetable stock

Salt and pepper to taste

Handful of fresh cilantro leaves, chopped, for garnish

Blanch the carrots and potatoes in salted boiling water until they start to soften. Drain. Heat the oil in saucepan over medium heat and sauté the onions, garlic, and chili until soft. Add the tomatoes, paprika, oregano, and parsley. Stir well.

Add the carrots, potatoes, and spinach. Sauté, stirring constantly, until the spinach wilts.

Add the corn and stock. Cover and simmer until the vegetables are nice and soft. Add salt and pepper, then lightly mash the carrots and potatoes into the sauce.

Serve garnished with the chopped cilantro and accompanied with crusty bread and a leafy green salad.

Bolivia in general is not great for vegetarians. La Paz is. Near the university I found possibly the best vegetarian restaurant in South America. However, the style of food in the vegetarian cafés was as much Californian as Bolivian. The best local dish I ate was a corn stew we had in a hillside restaurant on the way back from an exhilarating day out on the highest ski slope in the world.

This is a very tasty way of eating corn, which takes on all the flavors of the sauce in which it is cooked.

PERU

The jungles, deserts, mountains, and coast of Peru offer an abundance of exciting photographic opportunities, but a dearth of stimulating culinary experiences. Although many of the landscapes are well worth going a little hungry for, when we did find good food it was very welcome.

We entered Peru from Bolivia by ferry across Lake Titicaca in torrential rain. We were traveling through the Andes in midsummer — the wettest time of year. The floating reed islands of the Uros Indians out on the lake were soggy and decaying; the islanders looked bedraggled and unhappy. The only produce in the flooded vegetable market in Puno was rotting cilantro. Much of the railway line was under water, but we just managed to catch the last slow train over the altiplano.

Despite the weather, we walked the last day of the Inca Trail up to Machu Picchu, the spectacular "lost city of the Incas" hidden high in the Urubamba Valley. Later, I went back alone to the site at dawn. I climbed the tower of Wayna Picchu and looked down on the deserted city through the swirling clouds from the Temple of the Moon. Machu Picchu stays in my memory as one of the highlights of all my travels.

Dawn in the Andes

In Cuzco, better food and accommodations, the colonial splendors of the capital, and the dramatic ruins of Inca cities all combined to take our minds off the incessant rain. We ate these fried potato cakes with a vegetable filling and a spicy cucumber relish in the Plaza de Armas, where every evening women set up their food stalls.

POTATO CAKES WITH CUCUMBER RELISH

SERVES 4–6

2 pounds potatoes, peeled and cubed

About 3 tablespoons milk

3 tablespoons butter

Salt and pepper to taste

2 onions, finely chopped

2 fresh red Thai or serrano chilies, finely chopped

4 garlic cloves, crushed

Handful of cilantro stems, finely chopped

2 carrots, peeled and finely diced

2 red bell peppers, seeded, deribbed and finely diced

Oil for frying

Cucumber Relish

1 large cucumber, grated

2 fresh green Thai or serrano chilies, finely chopped

Handful of fresh cilantro leaves, finely chopped

Juice of 1 lemon

2 teaspoons honey

Salt to taste

Cook the potatoes in salted boiling water until soft. Drain and mash with a little milk and half the butter until smooth. Season to taste with salt and pepper.

Melt the remaining butter in a skillet over medium-low heat. Add the onions, red chilies, and garlic, and sauté until soft. Add the cilantro stems, carrots, and bell peppers, and sauté until soft.

Take a handful of the mashed potato, press an indentation into its center and fill with a little of the carrot and pepper mixture. Work the potato around to seal the stuffing and form into a cake with a diameter of about 3 inches. Repeat with the remaining potato and filling until all are used up. Fry the potato cakes in very hot oil in a nonstick skillet, until golden and crunchy on both sides.

Make the cucumber relish by combining all the ingredients.

Serve the potato cakes with the relish, any of the remaining carrot and pepper mixture, and a green salad. Alternatively, they are wonderful with poached eggs.

LIMA BEAN AND PUMPKIN STEW

SERVES 4–6

1 pounds potatoes, cubed

1 pound pie pumpkin, peeled, seeded, and cubed

4 tablespoons sunflower oil

2 onions, finely chopped

3 garlic cloves, crushed

1 jalapeño chili, minced

1 large ripe plum tomato, cubed

Leaves from handful of fresh thyme, minced

2 teaspoons ground cumin

1 cup cooked lima beans or butter beans

¼ cup fresh or frozen peas

¼ cup fresh or frozen corn kernels

Salt and pepper to taste

Handful of fresh parsley sprigs, minced, for garnish

1 cup (5 ounces) crumbled feta cheese, for garnish

Cook the potatoes and pumpkin in a saucepan of salted boiling water until they begin to soften. Drain, reserving the cooking water.

Heat the oil in a saucepan over medium heat and fry the onion, garlic, and chili until soft. Stir in the tomato, thyme, and ground cumin. Add the potatoes and pumpkin. Cook with a little of the reserved water for a couple of minutes.

Add the beans, peas, and corn and cook for 10 minutes. Add salt and pepper.

Serve sprinkled with the chopped parsley and feta cheese, accompanied with rice or crusty bread.

In Lima, we found relief from the rain that dogged our stay in Peru. The coastal deserts of Peru along the Pacific Ocean are some of the driest places on earth. Lima itself was a tense city with curfews every night.

We were staying with friends, who took us on day trips into the desert and out for fine meals in the evening. However, we found our most interesting Peruvian meal on a trip to the Cordillera Blanca Mountains. Along the mountain roads, women cooked stews on campfires. Among the bubbling pots of foul-smelling concoctions, we found a woman selling a lima bean and pumpkin stew. It was very good and set us up brilliantly for our trek into the hills.

Lima Bean and Pumpkin Stew

ECUADOR

The best dish we ate in Ecuador was a creamy pumpkin, potato, and paprika soup flavored with thyme and oregano. We were served it while staying on a ranch in the Andean foothills near the small town of Vilcabamba. The ranch was set in idyllic countryside, while Vilcabamba itself seemed like a Wild West town, with saddled horses tied up outside saloons, and drunks fighting in the town square. We saw a more elegant side of Ecuador in Cuenca, with its cathedral and its gleaming barber shops, well-stocked pharmacies, and tidy cafés around the main square.

For us, the highlight of Ecuador was the bustling market town of Otavalo, located at the foot of a volcano and populated by the best-looking, happiest-seeming, and most friendly Indians we met in all of South America. The men wore ponchos and wide-brimmed hats, the women attractive hooped skirts and lots of beads. We watched them play a traditional bat-and-ball game in the streets, although both the bat and the ball were so big that hitting the one with the other was almost impossible and most of the game seemed to be spent chasing after missed balls.

PUMPKIN SOUP

SERVES 4–6

3 tablespoons olive oil

1 onion, finely chopped

2 garlic cloves, crushed

1 heaped teaspoon sweet paprika

Leaves from 1 handful of fresh
    oregano, minced

12 ounces sweet potato, peeled and
    cubed

1 pound pie pumpkin, peeled,
    seeded, and cubed

2 cups vegetable stock

Salt and pepper to taste

½ cup heavy cream

Leaves from 1 handful of fresh thyme,
    minced, for garnish

Heat the olive oil in a saucepan over medium heat and sauté the onion until golden. Stir in the garlic, paprika, and oregano and sauté for 1 minute. Add the sweet potato and pumpkin and sauté until they start to soften. Add the stock and enough water to cover the vegetables. Bring to a boil, cover, and simmer until the vegetables are soft. Add salt and pepper.

In a food processor, blend the contents of the pan until smooth. Stir in the cream and serve garnished with thyme.

Along the outside of the Catholic cathedral in Cuenca, the walls are full of carved effigies in tiny alcoves

COSTA RICA

More than a quarter of Costa Rica is protected natural wilderness. The country's active policy of conservation and the immense biodiversity afforded by its tropical location has allowed "eco-tourism" to thrive. Areas of rain forest have been developed for visitors in a range of low-impact facilities, from campsites to the so-called "five-star rustic" resorts that offer a taste of the wildness of nature — but in comfort. This sounded seductive yet improbable, so we set out to discover just how "five-star" rustic can be, heading into the deep south where there are several remote resorts.

We decided to try the Tiskita Jungle Lodge, situated in 250 acres of virgin rain forest on the Pacific coast. Our accommodations consisted of a wooden cabin in the forest with an outdoor bathroom and a wide veranda looking out over the treetops and the ocean. The meals, eaten in the communal open-sided dining room, were excellent. The place was definitely more rustic than five-star, but quite comfortable and friendly. However, communing with nature does include sharing your bedroom with a lot more biodiversity than you'd ever expect in a hotel room — including, one night, an alarmingly large scorpion.

The daytime paradise easily made up for any nocturnal horrors. Troops of monkeys and parades of exotic birds and eccentric insects provided hours of entertainment as we sat on our veranda. But the real adventures were the forest walks. The trails were clear enough for us to wander off on our own and admire the giant plants, the towering liana-draped trees, the minute psychedelic-colored frogs around the forest pools, and a boa constrictor wrapped around a branch. Everywhere, the sounds of the forest were incredible: Unseen insects created an unruly racket, monkeys whooped and chattered, and birdsong filled the canopy.

Another attraction of Tiskita was experimental-fruit-orchard walks, on which we were urged to sample extraordinary offerings from a variety of trees. And there was yet more walking to enjoy along the miles of deserted black sand, palm-fringed beach, with the welcome relief of the foaming Pacific close at hand. The rain forest comes right down to the ocean, and here, looking back up at the vastness of the green forest or gazing out across the endless blue sea, we truly appreciated the blissful remoteness of our position and, as a pair of toucans glided overhead, the privilege of experiencing nature so unspoiled.

One of the beautiful untouched beaches of Costa Rica's Pacific coast

CRUNCHY SALAD WITH LIME JUICE

SERVES 4–6

1½ cups shredded cabbage

¾ cup diced cucumber

1 ripe mango, peeled, cut from the
    pit, and diced

1 red bell pepper, seeded, deribbed,
    and diced

6 green onions, thinly sliced

1 avocado, peeled, pitted, and cubed

2 handfuls of watercress, stemmed

Juice of 2 limes

1 garlic clove, crushed

3 tablespoons olive oil

Salt and pepper to taste

This fresh-tasting salad, with its sweet-and-sour mixture of fruit and vegetables, is typical of the dishes we sampled on the Pacific coast of Costa Rica.

Combine all the ingredients and mix well. Refrigerate for about 30 minutes before serving.

A short flight away on the Caribbean side of Costa Rica, we found a very different coast and an equally different cuisine. The recipe given here is a delicious mixture of sweet potatoes, pumpkin, and plantains in a rich mustard, coconut, and rum sauce.

Left Crunchy Salad with Lime Juice

Below Caribbean Vegetables in a Mustard, Coconut, and Rum Sauce

CARIBBEAN VEGETABLES IN A MUSTARD, COCONUT, AND RUM SAUCE

SERVES 4–6

2 onions, finely diced
4 garlic cloves
2-inch piece fresh ginger, peeled and coarsely chopped
2 teaspoons coriander seeds
½ teaspoon ground cloves
2-inch piece cinnamon stick
½ teaspoon cayenne pepper
2 teaspoons dry mustard
1 teaspoon ground turmeric
6 tablespoons sunflower oil
1 pound sweet potatoes, peeled and cubed
1 pound pie pumpkin or winter

squash, peeled, seeded, and cubed
4 tablespoons dark rum
1 cup vegetable stock
Water as needed
2 large plantains, peeled and cut into ½-inch slices
1¼ cups (14 ounces) coconut milk
Salt and pepper to taste
Juice of 1 lime
Minced fresh oregano for garnish
Mango slices for serving
Fresh chives, snipped into longish pieces, for garnish

In a food processor, blend the onions, garlic, and ginger to a paste. Using a spice grinder or mortar and pestle, grind the coriander seeds, cloves, and cinnamon. Add the cayenne, mustard, and turmeric.

Heat 4 tablespoons of the oil in a heavy saucepan over medium heat, add the onion paste, and fry for 2 minutes. Add the sweet potatoes and pumpkin or squash and fry until they start to soften. Add the spices and stir. Add the rum, then the stock. Cover and bring to a boil. Reduce heat to low, cover, and simmer with the lid on until the vegetables are tender. Add a little water, as necessary.

Meanwhile, fry the plantains in the remaining oil until brown and crunchy. Add the plantains to the saucepan with the coconut milk and simmer gently for 5 minutes. Add the salt, pepper, and lime juice.

Serve garnished with oregano, accompanied with the slices of fresh mango sprinkled with chives, and some rice.

MEXICO

The Mexican state of Oaxaca is a land of rugged mountains, ancient Zapotec and Mixtec ruins, Indian markets, and winding valleys around the preserved colonial gem of Cortez's southern capital of Oaxaca city. At the same time, as one of Mexico's west-coast states, it offers in places such as Puerto Escondido a very modern culture that owes little to its Aztec or Spanish past.

The city of Oaxaca is centered on the *zocalo* (square), a leafy oasis of shade surrounded by cafés under stone arcades. At night, each café has its own band of musicians to serenade customers, and street vendors offer bright plastic toys, giant balloons, multicolored candies, and armloads of hand-woven shawls. Every day at dawn and dusk, café society on the *zocalo* is silenced by a flamboyant display of nationalism as a troop of highly polished soldiers attends with great seriousness to the hoisting or lowering of the Mexican flag.

Beyond the *zocalo*, Oaxaca still retains much of its historic Andalusian charm. There are some fine sixteenth-century churches, the most impressive of which is Santo Domingo, with its lavish gold-leaf interior, where a Mass or even a wedding may take place oblivious to the gaze of visitors. The town is dotted with colonial haciendas constructed around tranquil courtyards; some of these have been converted into hotels and guesthouses, and we stayed in a charming example for several days.

Oaxaca's cuisine is part of the town's image and features heavily in its restaurants. *Oaxaqueño*, a stringy, mozzarella-style cheese, and mole, a rich, spicy chocolate and chili sauce, are both common. Slightly less so are *chapulines*, fried grasshoppers, which, even when cooked with onion and garlic and served with fresh lime, seemed like an acquired taste. Most of the ingredients, including piles of grasshoppers and blocks of raw chocolate, are on display in the Mercado de Abastos. In typical Mexican style, the market is a colourful labyrinth of stalls and shops, full of treats (and occasional horrors) for the eyes, nose, and stomach.

To the east of Oaxaca, we visited several ruins of Zapotec settlements, at Mitla enjoying a rare opportunity to see reasonably intact examples of original stone mosaic-work in geometric designs representing the elements – designs that are now used by weavers and potters. For all its subtle attractions, however, Mitla has none of the dramatic grandeur of its historic predecessor, Monte Albán. The ruins of this ancient city are majestically located just west of Oaxaca and 1,320 feet above it. Monte Albán at its peak, around 2,000 years ago, was home to 25,000 Zapotec inhabitants. The most

Piloncillo (unrefined sugar), and blocks of chocolate for making mole on sale in the market in Oaxaca

visible legacy of the settlement's architectural triumph is the flattened mountaintop on which the ruins stand. The mountain was leveled by hand to make a vast paved plateau. Around the edge, temples, tombs, palaces, platforms, and pyramids were constructed, and enough of them remain to make Monte Albán one of Mexico's finest relics of pre-Hispanic civilization.

From Oaxaca, we took an eight-seater plane back over the Sierra Madre to the coast to indulge in the relaxed pleasures of Puerto Escondido. The size and power of the waves along Zicatela Beach make a compelling spectacle, and attract surfers from all over the Americas. Surfing culture is also entertaining to observe. Surfing is a mainly male sport on Zicatela, and there is much strutting and posing to watch, as well as some extraordinary acrobatics and daring. The atmosphere is easy-going and inter-national. Puerto Escondido has none of the modern high-rise hotels found along the coast in Huatulco, nor is it as remote and laidback as the sleepy fishing village and one-time hippie hideaway of Puerto Angel, halfway between the two. Puerto Angel offers the ultimate wind-down after all the activity and urban formality of Oaxaca, and a chance to experience the Mexican *mañana* mood to the fullest.

GUACAMOLE

Smooth Guacamole

Serves 4–6

4 large ripe avocados (preferably
   Hass)
1 jalapeño chili, minced
Small handful of cilantro leaves,
   chopped, plus more for garnish

Juice of 1 lime
Salt to taste
Tortilla chips, for serving

Halve the avocados and pit them. Scoop out the flesh and put it in a food processor. Add the chili, cilantro, lime juice, and salt and blend until smooth.
   Serve garnished with cilantro and, accompanied with tortilla chips.

Chopped Guacamole

Serves 4–6

3 large ripe avocados (preferably
   Hass)
2 tomatoes, finely diced
1 small red onion, finely chopped
Juice of 1 lime

Salt to taste
Chopped fresh cilantro leaves for
   garnish
Tortilla chips, for serving

Peel and pit the avocados. Chop the flesh, place it in a bowl, and mash slightly with a fork. Add the tomatoes, onion, lime juice, and salt and mix well.
   Serve garnished with cilantro and accompanied with tortilla chips.

There are many different versions of guacamole, the delicious avocado salsa. It can be served smooth or with chopped avocado, so we've given you both options. You can serve it either as an appetizer or as an accompaniment.

Chopped Guacamole

This truly original dish combines chocolate and spices to make a rich, dark, savory sauce. We were taught this recipe by a woman in an Oaxacan market. She cooked everything on open fires in her court-yard, which her husband and sons also used as a mechanic's workshop. From tins and jars on shelves above dismantled engines and buckets of sump oil, she produced the dried ingredients, which she blended with the chocolate and other items to create the mole. We thanked her so enthusiastically for her trouble that she invited us to join her and the grinning mechanics for lunch. As our cookery lesson had been conducted next to an evil-smelling pot containing a boiling pig's head, we politely declined.

Oaxacan Mole

OAXACAN MOLE

It is best to use a chocolate with a high cocoa content.

SERVES 4–6

Mole Sauce

3 tablespoons roasted peanuts

¼ cup sesame seeds

¼ cup pumpkin seeds

2-inch piece cinnamon stick

⅔ cup ground almonds

1 level teaspoon ground allspice

½ teaspoon ground cloves

1 teaspoon dried thyme

1 level tablespoon dried oregano

1 onion, coarsely chopped

3 garlic cloves

2 jalapeño chilies

¼ cup raisins

1 banana, peeled and coarsely chopped

3 tablespoons sunflower oil

1 cup vegetable stock

4 ounces bittersweet chocolate

1 pound sweet potatoes, peeled and cut into 1-inch cubes

2 ears corn, cut into 1-inch rounds

4 tablespoons sunflower oil

2 plantains, peeled and cut into ½-inch-thick rounds

1 red and 1 yellow bell pepper, seeded, deribbed, and cut into 1-inch squares

4 ounces green beans

Salt to taste

1 cup water

To make the mole sauce: Grind the peanuts, sesame seeds, pumpkin seeds, and cinnamon together in a food processor. Add the ground almonds, allspice, cloves, thyme, oregano, onion, garlic, chillies, raisins, and banana. Blend to a thick paste. Heat the sunflower oil in a large saucepan over medium heat and fry the paste for 2 minutes, stirring constantly. Slowly add the stock, stirring well.

Add the chocolate to the sauce. Stir well until the chocolate has melted. Simmer gently for 10 minutes. The sauce will be quite thick.

Now prepare the vegetables: Blanch the sweet potatoes and corn in salted boiling water for 1–2 minutes. Drain well.

Heat the sunflower oil in a skillet over medium heat and fry the plantains until they start to brown. Add the sweet potatoes, corn, and peppers, and fry until they all start to brown.

Stir the fried vegetables into the mole sauce, then add the green beans and water. Simmer gently for 10 minutes. Season with salt.

REFRIED BEANS

When cooking beans it is important not to add salt until the end as salt stops them from softening properly.

SERVES 4–6

2 cups pinto beans, soaked in water overnight

1 level tablespoon cumin seeds

1 level tablespoon coriander seeds

4 tablespoons sunflower oil

1 large onion, finely chopped

Salt to taste

Drain and rinse the beans. Place in a large saucepan with fresh water to cover. Bring to a boil. A foam will rise to the surface of the pan; scoop it off and discard. Cover the pan and simmer until beans are tender. Drain.

Meanwhile, toast the cumin and coriander seeds in a hot skillet for 1 minute, stirring constantly. Grind in a spice grinder or using a pestle and mortar. Set aside.

Heat the sunflower oil in a skillet over medium heat and sauté the onion gently until soft (but not brown or it will be bitter). Add the ground spices and sauté with the onion for 1 minute, stirring constantly.

Add the onion mixture to the drained beans. Remove from the heat and mash with a potato masher until the beans are broken down. If necessary, add some broth to get a thick consistency. Add salt.

Beans are the staple of most Mexican meals. Refried beans are the most common and can be served with almost anything – the options are endless. They can be made with various beans, but pinto or black beans are the most common. We prefer to use pinto beans. In the café, we serve refried beans in a flour tortilla and as part of a mixed Mexican plate.

Above left **A colorful Oaxacan street**

Above **Hats for sale in the town of Mérida**

REFRIED BEANS WITH FLOUR TORTILLA

SERVES 1

1 serving Refried Beans (opposite page)

For the mixed salad
Finely shredded lettuce
Grated carrot
Finely shredded red cabbage
Finely shredded white cabbage

Lime juice
Olive oil
Chopped cilantro leaves for garnish
1 soft flour tortilla
Handful of shredded Monterey jack cheese
Dollop of sour cream

Reheat the refried beans. Combine all the salad ingredients and dress with the lime juice and olive oil. Sprinkle with the cilantro.

Toast the flour tortilla on a hot griddle or in a hot dry skillet until it starts to puff up. Turn and cover with cheese. When the cheese starts to melt, transfer it to a plate with the salad. Spoon the beans on the tortilla and fold it in half. Place a dollop of sour cream on top and serve immediately.

MEXICAN PLATE WITH REFRIED BEANS

SERVES 1

Mixed Salad (above recipe)
Fresh Tomato Salsa (page 176) or Salsa Ranchera (page 175)
Smooth Guacamole (page 168)
Dollop of sour cream
1 serving Refried Beans (opposite page)

Handful of shredded Monterey jack cheese
Chopped fresh cilantro leaves for garnish
Tortilla chips for serving

Arrange the salad on half of each plate and top it with servings of salsa, guacamole, and sour cream. Cover the remaining side of the plate with refried beans and top these with cheese. Garnish with chopped cilantro and place lots of tortilla chips around the edge of the plate. Serve immediately.

CHAYOTE IN A CINNAMON-SPICED TOMATO SAUCE

The chayote, a vegetable enjoyed all over Mexico, is now available in many supermarkets and produce stores. Resembling a large green pear, it is similar to summer squash in texture. The seed in the middle is considered a delicacy, so when chopping the chayote, use it all. If you cannot find chayote, use zucchini instead. When chayote is in season, we like to serve this dish garnished with zucchini flowers lightly fried in butter, together with mashed sweet potatoes to soak up the sauce.

SERVES 4–6

Tomato Sauce
4 tablespoons olive oil
1 large onion, diced
3 garlic cloves, crushed
1 teaspoon ground cinnamon
¼ teaspoon ground cloves
1 tablespoon tomato purée
1 pound tomatoes, finely diced
Handful of raisins
Large handful of fresh cilantro
    leaves, chopped
2 jalapeño chilies, minced

3 chayotes, peeled with a potato
    peeler and chopped into cubes,
    or 1½ pounds crookneck squash,
    cubed
5 baby zucchini, halved lengthwise
Salt and pepper to taste
Water as needed

Garnish (optional)
12 zucchini flowers
Butter, for sautéing
Salt and pepper to taste

To make the tomato sauce: Heat the olive oil in a saucepan over low heat and fry the onion and garlic until soft. Stir in the cinnamon and cloves, then add the tomato purée, diced tomatoes, raisins, cilantro, and chilies, together with a little water to thin the sauce. Simmer for 10 minutes.

Blanch the chayotes or squash and the zucchini in salted water until they start to soften. Drain and stir them into the sauce. Simmer gently for 15 minutes. Add salt and pepper.

If zucchini flowers are in season, gently sauté them in butter until they start to brown. Add salt and pepper.

Serve the dish garnished with the zucchini flowers, if you have them, and accompanied with sweet potatoes mashed with olive oil and minced fresh thyme.

On Saturdays, the streets and alleyways around the *mercado* in Oaxaca fill with Zapotec Indians from the surrounding countryside selling their produce on the pavement. As well as everyday goods, there are numerous Indian crafts on sale, including hundreds of blankets and rugs woven with traditional geometric patterns and colored with dyes such as cochineal and indigo.

Best of all, there's plenty of street food freshly prepared between the stalls to feed hungry shoppers. As well as lots of warm Oaxaqueño tortillas with various salsas, we ate a very good dish made with chayote, in a tomato, clove, and cinnamon sauce spiced with jalapenos and garlic.

When you order your food in Mexico, you will generally be asked if you would like red or green salsa. These are cooked salsas used to flavor your food. Take as little or as much as you like, but no meal is complete without them.

Our favorite is the red salsa known as salsa ranchera. A green version can be made by replacing tomatoes with tomatillos, which look like green tomatoes and are occasionally available in good supermarkets or produce markets. Salsa ranchera is also an ingredient in a favorite recipe of ours, Huevos Rancheros.

SALSA RANCHERA

SERVES 4–6

1–2 tablespoons sunflower oil
1 red onion, finely chopped
1 garlic clove, crushed
1–2 jalapeño chilies, minced

Handful of fresh cilantro leaves, chopped
6 tomatoes, finely diced
Salt to taste

Heat the oil in a small saucepan over low heat and sauté the onion and garlic until they start to soften. Stir in the chilies and cilantro and cook for a few more seconds. Add the chopped tomatoes and gently simmer until all the ingredients are soft and thickened. Season with salt.

This salsa can be stored in the refrigerator for up to 2 weeks.

HUEVOS RANCHEROS

Basically fried eggs served on a flour tortilla and covered in spicy ranchera sauce, this makes not only a delicious breakfast dish but also a wonderful lunch.

SERVES 1

1–2 soft flour tortillas
1–2 eggs
1 tablespoon olive oil
Salsa Ranchera (above), as much or as little as you like, but enough to cover the egg

Handful of shredded Monterey jack cheese
Chopped fresh cilantro leaves, for garnish

On a hot griddle or in a hot, dry skillet, cook the tortillas until they start to puff up. Flip them over and cook the other side.

Meanwhile, heat the oil in another skillet and fry the eggs, keeping the yolk soft. Heat the ranchera sauce.

Place a fried egg on top of each tortilla and cover with ranchera sauce. Sprinkle with cheese and cilantro. Serve immediately.

FRESH TOMATO SALSA

This fresh tomato salsa is often eaten with tortilla chips as an appetizer. It is also good served with refried beans.

SERVES 4–6

1 small red onion, coarsely chopped.

1–2 jalapeño chilies

Large handful of fresh cilantro leaves, chopped, plus more for garnish

5 ripe tomatoes, coarsely chopped

Juice of 2 limes

Salt to taste

Tortilla chips, for serving

Chop the onion, chilies, and cilantro in a food processor until finely chopped (you can do this by hand if you prefer). Add the tomatoes, lime juice, and salt, then briefly blend again until the tomatoes are finely chopped and blended with all ingredients, but not turned to tomato juice.

Serve garnished with more chopped cilantro and accompanied with tortilla chips, or as an accompaniment to any meal.

FRESH TOMATO AND RADISH SALSA

This is a chunkier salsa, which again may be served with tortilla chips or to accompany any meal.

SERVES 4–6

4 tomatoes, finely diced

1 small red onion, finely diced

1 bunch radishes, sliced

Small handful of fresh cilantro leaves, chopped

Juice of 1 lime

Salt to taste

1 small green Thai or serrano chili, minced

Mix all the ingredients together.

As well as the cooked salsas served as condiments, there are various fresh salsas made with raw ingredients, which may be served as an appetizer or as an accompaniment to the main dish.

Fresh Tomato and Radish Salsa

FRESH FRUIT SALSA

Surfers in the sunset at
Puerto Escondido

*In Oaxaca city, market stalls are piled high with the most beautiful fruits — papaya,
watermelon, and cantaloupe are but a few — and these are often used to make a spicy
salsa.*

SERVES 4–6

½ cup pumpkin seeds
1 pound papaya, watermelon,
    honeydew melon, or cantaloupe,
    or a combination, peeled, seeded,
    and diced

Juice of 2 limes
Handful of fresh cilantro leaves
1 jalapeño chili, minced
Salt to taste

Toast the pumpkin seeds in a hot skillet until they become golden, stirring
constantly. Set aside to cool.

Mix your choice of fruit with the lime juice, cilantro, and chili. Season with
salt and sprinkle with the toasted pumpkin seeds.

In Puerto Escondido, New Age Californian culture blends with local Oaxacan youth culture on the surf beaches and in their cafés. This blend has crept into the food. The beach cafés open at dawn to serve surfers as much with muesli, fresh fruit, and yogurt as with huevos rancheros. By midday, the choice expands to all manner of vegetarian, fish, and meat dishes. Many cafés serve Indonesian tempeh. The recipe given here combines tempeh with colorful peppers, olives and that Mexican staple, pinto beans.

MEXICAN WEST COAST PEPPERS

Serves 4–6

5 tablespoons olive oil

10 ounces tempeh, cut into ½-inch cubes

2 red onions, thinly sliced

4 garlic cloves, sliced

2 fresh red Thai or serrano chilies, chopped

2 tablespoons coriander seeds, crushed

2 red bell peppers, 2 yellow bell peppers and 1 green bell pepper, seeded, deribbed, and sliced

1¼ cups cooked pinto beans

24 black olives, pitted and halved

Soy sauce to taste

Large handful of fresh cilantro leaves, chopped

Heat half the oil in a large skillet over medium heat and sauté the tempeh until brown. Remove the tempeh from the pan and set aside.

Add the remaining oil to the pan and sauté the onions until they start to soften. Add the garlic, chilies, and crushed coriander. Sauté for a couple of minutes.

Add the peppers and sauté, stirring regularly, until they start to soften. Add the pinto beans and olives. When the beans are heated through, return the tempeh to the pan and stir well.

Add the soy sauce and cilantro. Serve immediately with Fresh Fruit Salsa (opposite page) and rice.

CUBA

There was only one flight a week between London and Havana in the winter of 1994, and that was on a rather old and ill-equipped Russian airplane operated by Cubana out of Stansted Airport. The lack of in-flight entertainment was partly compensated for by the freely available Havana Club rum. The biggest shock was a stopover in the frozen north of Canada, where we had to endure sub-zero temperatures as we walked to and from the terminal building, dressed for the Caribbean in T-shirts and sandals.

It can be uncomfortable arriving in a strange city at night with no accommodations booked. But, far from being besieged by taxi drivers competing to whisk us into the unknown for a huge fare, we found the Havana Airport taxi-men playing guitars under a tree in the tropical evening. After a sedate drive down almost empty roads at a fixed fare to the heart of Old Havana, we found a fine room in a hotel rich, like Havana itself, in faded splendor. The elegant Spanish colonial architecture, the brightly colored 1950s American cars, the post-revolutionary street art, the subtle pastels of the back alleys, and the friendly Cuban people — all made photography a pleasure. Eating was another matter. Seduced into restaurants by stunning interiors and smiling staff, we inevitably found nothing to back up the optimistic words on the menus, while the big hotels seemed content to serve dishes reminiscent of boarding-school meals of the 1960s. We were beginning to despair when rescue came from what seemed a most unlikely source.

At first, we had been rather intimidated by the gangs of young men hustling to sell dubious merchandise in the shadows. But after a couple of days, we discovered that they were much less threatening than they appeared, and in fact quite friendly and keen to chat in English. Having turned down their suggestions of various substances to smoke, sniff, or sip, we found they had something else to offer. A boy who introduced himself as José was our guide to this elusive pleasure. Reluctant at first to follow him down the quiet, narrow streets into the midst of Old Havana's decay, we nonetheless stayed close behind him, drawn by his promise of tasty, home-cooked Cuban dishes for a few dollars.

José introduced us to Rosa, his aunt. Rosa was an old hand at saving foreigners from Havana's dearth of nutritious satisfaction. With her passion for traditional Cuban cooking, she provided some of our most pleasant and enduring memories of Cuba. After her delicious meals, we would spend the warm Havana nights sipping Mojito rum cocktails in one of the foodless bars or cafés, followed by live Afro-Cuban dance music at an open-air club, against a background of Atlantic waves crashing on the shore.

One of the many big old American cars to be seen on the streets of Havana

CUBAN GREEN RICE

SERVES 4–6

3 tablespoons olive oil
1 large onion, finely chopped
1 green bell pepper, seeded deribbed, and finely chopped
Large handful of fresh parsley sprigs, chopped

Large handful of fresh cilantro leaves, chopped
2 cups rice, rinsed and drained
2½ cups vegetable stock
Salt and pepper to taste

Heat the oil in a medium saucepan over medium heat and sauté the onion and bell pepper until they start to soften.

Stir in the parsley and cilantro. Add the rice and stir to coat all the grains in oil. Add just enough stock to cover the rice and bring to a boil, then reduce the heat to low, cover, and cook until all the moisture is absorbed. Add salt and pepper.

HAVANA BEANS

Serves 4–6

1½ cups dried black beans, soaked
    overnight in cold water

6 tablespoons olive oil

2 large red onions, thinly sliced

6 garlic cloves, crushed

2 red bell peppers, seeded,
    deribbed, and thinly sliced

2 yellow bell peppers, seeded,
    deribbed and thinly sliced

1 pound cabbage, cored and finely
    shredded

Large handful of cilantro stems,
    chopped, and a large handful of
    chopped fresh cilantro leaves

Large handful of oregano leaves,
    minced, plus more for garnish

Tabasco sauce to taste

5 tablespoons red wine

Salt and pepper to taste

Garnish

Minced fresh oregano

Slices of plum tomato

Olive oil for drizzling

Drain the beans, add enough fresh water to cover generously, bring to a boil, and simmer until soft. Drain the beans, retaining the broth.

Meanwhile, heat 4 tablespoons of the olive oil in a large saucepan over medium heat and sauté the red onions and garlic until they start to soften. Add the red and yellow bell peppers, then the cabbage. Sauté, stirring constantly, until the vegetables are tender and caramelized.

Add the cilantro stems, oregano, and Tabasco – it should be quite spicy! Stir well and add the wine. Cook to reduce the wine by about half. Add the cooked beans and the remaining olive oil, followed by enough of the reserved bean broth to make a sauce. Simmer for 5 minutes.

Add the salt, pepper, and cilantro. Stir until well incorporated.

Serve immediately, garnished with oregano, and accompanied with Cuban Green Rice (page 181) and plum tomato slices drizzled with olive oil.

CHOCOLATE CAKE

In nearly all the countries we have traveled in, the most common dessert is fresh fruit. However, in the café we serve a French chocolate cake, which is probably our most requested recipe. Up to now we have always tried to keep it a secret, but this book would not be complete without it.

SERVES 8–10

7 ounces bittersweet plain
    chocolate, broken into pieces
1 cup (2 sticks) unsalted butter, plus
    more for the cake pan
6 large eggs, separated

1 cup granulated sugar
Confectioners' sugar for dusting
Crème fraîche and fresh
    strawberries for serving

Preheat the oven to 375°F. Butter a 9-inch springform pan.

In a small saucepan set over a larger pan of simmering water, melt the chocolate and butter. Mix together well and set aside to cool.

Beat the egg whites until stiff, glossy peaks form. Gradually whisk in the granulated sugar, then the egg yolks. The result will be a creamy mixture.

Fold the chocolate mixture into the egg mixture. Pour and spoon into the prepared pan.

Bake for about 55 minutes. The cake will puff up in the oven but will sink back down again when removed from the heat, giving it its characteristic appearance.

Dust with confectioners' sugar and serve with crème fraîche and strawberries.

Chocolate Cake

GLOSSARY OF INGREDIENTS

amchoor Made from ground dried unripe mango, this powder gives food a sweet sourness. It is available from Indian stores.

asafetida See *hing*.

bindi See *okra*.

black bean paste A paste of puréed, salted, and fermented soybeans, available from good supermarkets or Chinese stores. Alternatively you can buy the black beans whole, rinse them and purée them with some water.

"Buddhist meat" A delicious meat substitute made from marinated wheat gluten, this is available from health-food stores under the name of seitan.

bulgur (bulghur) wheat Cracked kernels of wheat, available in fine or medium coarseness (we prefer fine). It can be bought from good supermarkets or health-food stores.

cardamom Aromatic pods containing either green or black seeds. Remove the seeds from the pod for maximum flavor; alternatively it is possible to buy the seeds or ground seeds only.

cassava A Brazilian root vegetable similar to a large sweet potato but with a darker skin. Its flesh is hard and white, but becomes glutinous when cooked.

coconut milk Available canned, powdered, or creamed. We like the canned form best. It is thicker than the powdered version and less likely to separate on being cooked. If you do use the powder, always mix it to a consistency thicker than that suggested on the packet. The creamed coconut, sold in blocks, tends to be rather oily.

curry leaves Highly aromatic leaves much used in Indian cooking. Shaped like small bay leaves, they are much better fresh than dried, and fresh leaves can be bought from Indian stores. Dried are available from supermarket spice counters. Curry leaves can be frozen.

daikon See *mooli*.

galangal This root, a member of the ginger family, is available fresh or dried from Thai, Chinese or Malaysian stores. If necessary, root ginger makes a good substitute.

ghee Well-clarified butter, used in Indian cooking and available from Indian stores or good supermarkets. It is possible to buy a dairy-free version.

gram flour Made from ground chickpeas, this flour is available from good supermarkets or Indian stores.

hing Also known as asafetida, this pungent resin flavoring, ground into a yellow powder, is available from Indian stores.

hoisin sauce A dark brown, sweet, smooth Chinese bean sauce, available from good supermarkets or Chinese stores.

jaggery Lump brown sugar from a type of palm tree, jaggery is sold in blocks in Indian stores and sometimes also in the ethnic sections of good supermarkets.

jalapeño chilies The most commonly used chilies in Mexico, these are available fresh, dried, or canned in brine, from good supermarkets or speciality stores. Jalapeño chilies are large and quite hot; if using regular chilies double the quantity.

lemongrass These hard, thick, pale-green stalks are much used in Southeast Asian cooking. Their distinctive lemon flavor is best brought out by bruising the stalks with a rolling pin before adding them to the pot. It is possible to buy lemongrass fresh, freeze-dried whole, or dried and sliced or dried and ground. If you use dried, 2 tablespoons is equivalent to 1 stalk; but try to use fresh when possible. Lemongrass stalks can be frozen, so stock up your freezer whenever you can. They are available from good supermarkets and Chinese, Thai, or Malaysian stores.

lime leaves The leaves of the kaffir lime tree, widely used in Southeast Asian cooking. They are available from Thai, Chinese, or Malaysian stores.

mooli A large white radish with a mild flavor, available from good supermarkets and Chinese or Thai stores. Also known as daikon.

mung dal Split mung beans, available from Indian stores.

okra Finger-length, green, podlike vegetables, also known as bindi, and available from good supermarkets and Indian, Chinese, or Thai stores.

paneer An Indian fresh cheese, white in color and available in blocks from good supermarkets or Indian stores. Quite bland on its own, paneer is tasty when cooked in sauces.

pinto beans These medium-sized dried beans flecked with brown and pink are available from health-food stores or good supermarkets.

plantain This tropical fruit looks like a large thick-skinned green banana and it is related to the banana, although it is quite different in flavor and texture.

rose water Water flavored with roses is available from Middle Eastern stores, delicatessens, or good supermarkets.

seitan See *"Buddhist meat."*

tahini (tahina) A thick paste made from ground hulled sesame seeds, and available from health-food stores, good supermarkets, delicatessens, or Middle Eastern stores.

tamarind These brown pods used as a sour flavoring can be bought dried or as a ready-made purée or concentrate. We prefer tamarind purée, which is available from good supermarkets, Indian stores, or health-food shops. Tamarind concentrate is indeed much more concentrated and half the quantity stated in the recipe is usually sufficient. If you can only get the dried pods,

soak them in boiling water for 1 hour, or simmer them in water until soft, then pass through a sieve to collect the tamarind water and pulp. Use both, discarding the pods and the pips.

tempeh A nutty-flavored brown block made from soybeans, available from health-food or Indonesian stores.

tofu Made from set soybean curd, tofu is available in many forms, including soft, hard, deep-fried, marinated, and smoked. We like to use deep-fried tofu, as it has more flavor and needs little cooking.

tomato purée A preparation of smooth, thick, sieved tomatoes, available from good supermarkets, delicatessens, and health-food stores.

tortillas, flour Soft Mexican pancakes, tortillas are at the center of most Mexican meals. They are available from good supermarkets, delicatessens, or health-food stores.

INDEX

Recipe page numbers are
indexed in **bold** type,
illustration page numbers in *italic*

A

accompaniments to dishes 9, 145
  see also cachumber, chutney,
      dip, harissa, relish, salsa,
      sambal, sombol,
      side dish, raita
Adam's Peak 102, *107*
Africa
  East 46–53
  West 42–3
aloo gobi 61
  of Rajasthan **90**
Andes *156*, 160
Annapurna *100*
  ~ dal bhaat **101**
apple salad, sweet **55**, *57*
Aqabah 26, 33
Arabs, Arabic 14, 26, 47
  see also Bedouin
arugula
  and grated carrot salad **28**
  salad, Jordanian **33**
asparagus 118, 122
Atlas Mountains 12, 20
avocado 168

B

baba ghanoush **33**
Badami 76, **79**
Bali 143, *144*
  Balinese gado gado *142*, **143**
banana raita **85**, 93
Bandar Seri Begawan *137*
Bangalore 76
Bangkok 128–9
  ~ stir-fry **129**
batura bread 81

beans
  ful medames **28**, *29*
  Havana ~ **183**
  refried ~ **172, 173**
  West African ~ **42**
  white beans 34
  see also black, lima
Bedouin 14, 26–7
beet 93
  ~ and brinjal black curry **106**
  ~ salad **28**
berberé paste 13, **48**
Berbers 14
besan (gram flour) 95
black bean paste 136
black bean stew **152**, *153*
bok choy 118
Bolivia 154–5, *154*
Borneo 134, *135*
  ~ rain forest vegetables
      140, *141*
Brazil 148-9, 150-3, *150*
bread 12, 13, 14, 26, 42,
    49, 60
  batura bread 81
  see also pita bread
breadfruit 56
brinjal see eggplant
briouats 14
broccoli 104, 122
Brunei 134, *135, 137*
"Buddhist meat" 151
  ~ and shiitake mushrooms
      121
bulgur wheat 31
Burma 116–19, *117*
butternut squash 56

C

cabbage 37
  coconut **79**

red 93
cachumbers **78**
cake *see* chocolate
Calcutta 70, *72*
Calcutta eggplant **72**, *73*
Caribbean vegetables in a
    mustard, coconut, and rum
    sauce **165**, *165*
carri coco curry **56**, *57*
carrot 20
  salad **25, 96**
cashew nuts 64, 140
cassava 56
  and celery in mung dal gravy
      52
cauliflower 64, 90, 122
cayenne pepper 13, 64
chana
  batura, masala 81
  in a thick, spicy gravy **81**
chayote in a cinnamon-spiced
    tomato sauce **174**
cheese 88
chermoula 24
chickpeas 16, 32, 35, 81
chilies 8, *36*, 61, 104
  chili paste (harissa) 12, **22**
  see also berberé paste,
      sambal, sombol
China *112–13, 120–23*
Chinese leaf 55, 56, 118
chocolate *167, 171*
  chocolate cake **184**, *185*
chutney 76, 84–5
  green coconut **84**
  sweet date and tamarind **84**
  toasted coconut **108**
  tomato and cinnamon **23**
cilantro 24
Cochin coconut masala **82**
coconut 13, 47, 56, 60, 76, 98,
    104, 107

  ~ and pineapple chutney,
      toasted ~ **108**
  ~ cabbage **79**, 97
  chutney, green ~ **84**
  Kuching tamarind and
      coconut milk curry **139**
  masala, Cochin ~ **82**
  ~ rice 106, **108**
  ~ sambol 109, **111**
corn
  curry **98**, *99*
  ~ stew **155**
couscous 12, 14
  Ouarzazate **20**
Costa Rica 162–5, *163*
Covent Garden 8
cozido **151**
Creole 13, 55-6
crunchy salad with lime juice
    164, *164*
crunchy sweet-and-sour
    salad **126**, *127*
Cuba 180–83, *181*
Cuban green rice **181**
cucumber 25
  ~ and mint raita **85**
  ~ and sesame seed salad **116**
  ~ relish **157**
curry
  beet and brinjal black ~
      106
  carri coco ~ **56**
  Diu corn ~ **98**
  jungle ~ **130**
  Kandy leek and potato ~
      109
  Kuching tamarind and
      coconut milk ~ **139**
  Thai green ~ **132**
  vegetable mallung **104**
curry paste, green **132**
Cuzco 157

D

Dades valley 20, *23*
dairy products 8, 40
Dal Lake *66*
dal (lentils)
 ~ bhaat **101**
 fried ~ **63**
 mung ~ 52
dates 14, 41
date and tamarind chutney **84**, 97
deep-red Rajasthani vegetables
 in a poppy-seed sauce *92*, **93**
Delhi 86
desert 26, *27*
Diafarabe *10–11*, **42**
Didyma *38*
dip, eggplant **33**
Diu corn curry **98**, *99*
Divali
 (Festival of Lights) 70
Djenné *13*, 42

E

East Africa 46-53
Ecuador 160-61, *161*
eggplant 18, 125, 129
 baba ghanoush **33**
 beet and brinjal black curry
  106
 Calcutta ~ **72**
 in date sauce **41**
 imam's ~ **37**
 Mekong stir-fry **125**
 Thai green curry **132**
 in yogurt **66**
Egypt 12, 26-35
Ethiopia 13, 48-9
Ethiopian vegetable wat **49**

F

falafel 25, 31, **32**
fish 8, 24, 47, 56

fish paste 104
France, the French, French-
 speaking 14, 42, 54, 124, 184
frankincense 40
French chocolate cake **184**, *185*
fresh fruit salsa **178**
fresh tomato salsa **176**
fresh tomato and radish salsa
 176, *177*
fried dal **63**
fruit and vegetable salad **137**
fruit lassi **83**
ful medames **28**, *29*
Fulani 42

G

gado gado 134, *142*, **143**
Galle 106
Ganesh *80*
Ganges, River *71*
ghee 60
ginger *13*
Giza *27*
gluten, wheat 121
Gopalpur *74*
gram flour 95
green coconut chutney **84**
green curry paste **132**
green-vegetable mallung
 104, *105*
guacamole **168**, *169*
Gujarat 86, 88, 98
Gujarati carrot salad **96**, 98
Gujarati pumpkin with
 tamarind **97**, 98
Gulf, the 12

H

Hampi 76
harira soup 14, **16**
harissa (chili paste) 12, 18, 21, **22**
Havana 180

~ beans **183**
Hong Kong 120–21
hoppers 111
Huang Shan *112–13*, *123*
huevos rancheros **175**
hummus 31, **35**

I

imam's eggplant **37**
India *58–9*, *60–61*, *61*
 Eastern 70–75
 Northern 62–7
 Southern 76–85
 Western 86–99
Indian Ocean 13
Indonesia 135–145
Indonesian sambal **145**
Iran, the Iranians
 see Persia
Irrawaddy River 116, *117*
Istanbul 36

J

Jebel Akhdar Mts. 40, *41*
Jodhpur *91*
jollof rice, West African **43**
Jordan 26–35
Jordanian arugula salad *29*, **33**
jungle curry **130**, *131*

K

Kandy leek and potato curry **109**
Karnataka 76
kasbah (citadel) 20, *23*
Kashmir 62, *62*
kashmiri gobi **64**, *65*
Kenya 46
Kerala 76
khadi 95
Kuching tamarind and coconut
 milk curry **139**

L

La Digue (Seychelles) 13,
 54–7, *55*
Lamu 46
Laos 124–7
La Paz *154*
lassi 83
Lawrence of Arabia 26
leeks 109
lemons 36
 preserved ~ **22**, *22*
lemongrass rice **117**
lentil 13
 ~ soup **34**
 see also dal
Levant, the 12, 26–35
lima bean and pumpkin stew
 158, *159*
Luxor *35*

M

Machu Picchu 156
Maghreb, the 22
Malaysia 8, 13, 135–45, *145*
 Malay sambal **138**
 Malaysian fruit and vegetable
  salad **137**
 Malaysian sambal **145**
Mali *13*, 42–5
mallung, green-vegetable **104**,
 105
mango 83
 ~ salsa **152**
market places *12, 15, 17, 26,*
 61, 90
Marrakesh 14, *15*, *19*
 ~ tagine **18**, *19*
marrow 104
Masai *46*
masala
 chana ~ **81**
 Cochin coconut ~ **82**
 mixed vegetable ~ **75**

mashed carrot salad **39**
meat 8, 14, 40, 43, 48, 51, 150
Mediterranean 12
Mekong stir-fry with
   puréed eggplant **125**
mela (fair)
   camel (Pushkar) *86, 87, 94*
   elephant (Sonepur) *70*
mensaf (whole sheep) 12, 26
Mexico 9, 166–79, *167, 172, 178*
Mexican plate with refried
   beans **173**
Mexican West Coast peppers **179**
meze 31, 37
mint tea **15**
mixed-vegetable masala **75**
Mkomazi cardamom-mashed
   sweet potatoes with pepper
   relish **50**, *51*
mole 166
   Oaxacan ~ *170,***171**
Moors 14
Moroccan mixed salad plate **25**
Morocco *12,* 12, 14–25
mosques *13*
mushrooms *see* shiitake

N
Nalagarh 64, 67
   ~ brinjal 64, **66**
narangi pulao *66,* **67**
Neal's Yard 8
Nepal 61, 100–101
Niger, River *10–11, 42, 43,* **44**
Nile, River 26
noodles 139

O
Oaxaca *9,* 166, *167*
   Oaxacan mole *170,* **171**
okra 13, 42

olives, olive oil *12,* 14, *15,* 25, 36
Oman 12, 40–41, 67
onion sambol **111**
orange rice 64, **67**
Orissa 74
Orissan jagdish saag aloo **74**
Ottoman Empire 36
Ouarzazate 14, *21*
   ~ couscous **20**

P
Pagan 116, 118
paneer 60, 88
Patna 70
pawa (flat rice) 78
peanuts 13
   peanut sauce **143**
pepper relish **50**, *50*
Persia, the Persians 67
Peru 156–9, *156*
Petra 26, *30*
pineapple 108
piri-piri 13
pitta bread 26, 32, 33
plantain 13
poppy-seed sauce 93
Portugal, the Portuguese 13, 98
potato 67
   aloo gobi 60, **90**
   and leek curry **109**
   and peanut pawa **78**
   ~ bondas *68,* **69**
   ~ cakes with cucumber
      relish **157**
   saag aloo **74**
potatoes, sweet
   see sweet potatoes
preserved lemons **22**, *22*
Puerto Escondido *167, 178*
pumpkin 20, 93, 97, 151, 158
   ~ soup **160**

Pushkar 86, *87, 94*
pyramids *27*

R
rain forest *135, 150,* 151, 162
   ~ vegetables **140**, 141
raita 76, **85**, 88
Rajasthan 86, 88, 90, *90,* 93
Ramadan 16
Rangoon 116, *117*
refried beans **172**
   ~ with flour tortilla **173**
   Mexican plate with **173**
relish 50
   cucumber ~ **157**
rice 9, 60, 76, 100, *120*
   coconut **108**
   Cuban green ~ **181**
   lemongrass ~ **117**
   orange ~ **67**
   pawa **78**
   rose water ~ **40**
   West African jollof ~ **43**
Rio de Janeiro *146–7,* 150
root vegetables in a spicy
   mint sauce **91**
rose water 12
   ~ rice **40**
roti (bread) 111
Royal Geographical Society
   26, 46, 134, 150

S
saag paneer 88, *89*
Sahara, Sahel 12, 42
salad 26
   arugula and grated carrot ~
      28
   beet **28**
   carrot ~ **25, 96**
   crunchy ~, with lime juice
      164, *164*

crunchy sweet-and-sour ~
   126
cucumber and sesame seed ~
   116
Jordanian arugula ~ **33**
Malaysian fruit and
   vegetable ~ **137**
mashed carrot ~ **39**
plate, Moroccan mixed ~ **25**
savory fruit ~ **95**
spicy bean curd and
   bean sprout ~ **133**
sweet apple ~ **55**, *57*
tomato and cucumber ~ **28**
tomato, cucumber, and
   green pepper ~ **37**
white bean ~ **34**
see also meze
salsa 150
   fresh fruit ~ **178**
   fresh tomato ~ **176**
   fresh tomato and radish ~
      176, *177*
   mango ~ **152**
   ~ ranchera **175**
sambal **138**, *145*
sambol **111**
samosas 61
Saunders, Nicholas 8
satay 134
savory fruit salad **95**
seafood 8
seitan, *see* gluten, wheat
Seychelles 13, 54–7, *55*
shiitake mushrooms 121
Singapore 136
Somali coast 12, 13
souk, *see* marketplaces
soup
   harira ~ **16**
   lentil ~ **34**
   pumpkin ~ **160**
South China stir-fry **122**
spices 8-9

spicy bean curd and bean sprout
    salad **133**
spicy garlic-fried green
    vegetables **136**
spinach 55
    saag aloo **74**
    saag paneer **88**, *89*
squash
    see butternut squash
Sri Lanka 61, 102-111, *103,
    107, 110*
stir-fry
    Bangkok ~ **129**
    Mekong ~ **125**
    South China ~ **122**
    spicy green vegetables **136**
~ with tamarind gravy **118**,
    119
street food *17*, 32, 33, 60,
    129, 136, *145*
Sukhothai *129*, 130
sweet apple salad **55**, *57*
sweet date and tamarind
    chutney **84**
sweet potatoes 13, 47, 56
    ~ in cayenne, ginger, and
        peanut sauce 43, **44**, *45*

T
tabbouleh *29*, **31**
tagine (stew) 12, 14, **18**, *19*
tahini 32
tamarind 84, 97, 118
    ~ and coconut milk curry
        139
Tamil Nadu 76
Tanzania 46, *46*
tea 15, 27
tempeh 140, 143, 179
    ~ goreng and bean sprouts
        144
Thai green curry **132**
Thailand 128–133, *129*

thali 60, 76
Tibet 62
Tioman Island 138
toasted coconut and pineapple
    chutney 106, **108**
tofu 121, 133, 151
tomato 16, 24, 25, 37, 78
    ~ and cinnamon chutney **23**
    ~ and cucumber salad **28**
    ~ cucumber, and green
        pepper **37**
    salsa, fresh ~ **176**
Turkey 12, 36-9
turnip 20

U
Udaipur 88, 91

V
Varanasi 70, *71*
Vientiane *124, 127*

W
wat (Ethiopian stew) 48-9
    vegetable *wat* **49**
West African jollof rice **43**
West African beans and okra
    42
white bean salad **34**
Worcestershire sauce 104
World Food Café 8, 28, 31,
    37, 44, 56, 60, 61

Y
yogurt
    eggplant in ~ **66**
    fruit lassi **83**
    khadi **95**
    ~ with cucumber **39**
    see also raita

Z
Zanzibar *9*, 13, 46
    ~ beans in coconut sauce **47**
Zapotec Indians 166–7, 174

ACKNOWLEDGMENTS

Many people have helped to make this book happen, whether by creating opportunities, offering hospitality, giving recipes or sharing adventures. We especially wish to thank Nigel de Winser, Joana Scadden, Cecilia Weston-Baker, John Grain, Kirsty Seymour-Ure, Donna and Simon Leibowitz, Christine Dunk, Sally Cracknell, Vicky Mitchell, Satish Jacob and family, Vijayendra Singh and family, Kishori and Kalpa Shah, John and Richard Hunt, Robert Spensly, Daniel Tucker, Sophie Chamier and Giles Caldicott.
Map of the world copyright © AND Cartographic Publishers Ltd.

Commissioning Editor
Jo Christian

Managing Art Editor
Jo Grey

Text Editor
Kirsty Seymour-Ure

Art Editor
John Grain

Recipe Editor
Lewis Esson

Food Styling
Nicola Fowler

Editorial Assistance
**Sophie Lynch,
Tom Armstrong
and Tom Windross**

Production
Hazel Kirkman

Picture Editor
Anne Fraser

Indexer
Roger Owen

Art Director
Caroline Hillier

Editorial Director
Kate Cave